T0316750

CAMBRIDGE LIBRARY COLLECTION

Books of enduring scholarly value

British and Irish History, Nineteenth Century

This series comprises contemporary or near-contemporary accounts of
the political, economic and social history of the British Isles during the
nineteenth century. It includes material on international diplomacy and
trade, labour relations and the women's movement, developments in
education and social welfare, religious emancipation, the justice system,
and special events including the Great Exhibition of 1851.

Proposals for an Economical and Secure Currency

David Ricardo's work on currency was published in 1816, and this second
edition appeared in the same year. Enormously successful as a stockbroker,
Ricardo (1772–1823) was able to lead the life of a wealthy country squire,
while his intellectual interests caused him to move in the circles of Thomas
Malthus and James Mill. Written at the urging of the Cornish businessman
Pascoe Grenfell, M.P., who shared Ricardo's interest in financial matters,
this work considers the problem of the national debt, in the context of paper
money and whether it should in principle be exchanged at face value for
gold bullion rather than for minted coins. Ricardo was very concerned at
the large profits being made by the Bank of England in its dealings with
the government, and suggests here the creation of an independent central
bank, a proposal to which he later returned.

Cambridge University Press has long been a pioneer in the reissuing of out-of-print titles from its own backlist, producing digital reprints of books that are still sought after by scholars and students but could not be reprinted economically using traditional technology. The Cambridge Library Collection extends this activity to a wider range of books which are still of importance to researchers and professionals, either for the source material they contain, or as landmarks in the history of their academic discipline.

Drawing from the world-renowned collections in the Cambridge University Library and other partner libraries, and guided by the advice of experts in each subject area, Cambridge University Press is using state-of-the-art scanning machines in its own Printing House to capture the content of each book selected for inclusion. The files are processed to give a consistently clear, crisp image, and the books finished to the high quality standard for which the Press is recognised around the world. The latest print-on-demand technology ensures that the books will remain available indefinitely, and that orders for single or multiple copies can quickly be supplied.

The Cambridge Library Collection brings back to life books of enduring scholarly value (including out-of-copyright works originally issued by other publishers) across a wide range of disciplines in the humanities and social sciences and in science and technology.

Proposals for an Economical and Secure Currency

*With Observations on the Profits of the Bank of England,
as They Regard the Public and the Proprietors of Bank Stock*

DAVID RICARDO

CAMBRIDGE
UNIVERSITY PRESS

CAMBRIDGE
UNIVERSITY PRESS

University Printing House, Cambridge, CB2 8BS, United Kingdom

Cambridge University Press is part of the University of Cambridge.
It furthers the University's mission by disseminating knowledge in the pursuit of
education, learning and research at the highest international levels of excellence.

www.cambridge.org
Information on this title: www.cambridge.org/9781108075459

© in this compilation Cambridge University Press 2015

This edition first published 1816
This digitally printed version 2015

ISBN 978-1-108-07545-9 Paperback

Second Edition.

PROPOSALS

FOR AN

ECONOMICAL AND SECURE

CURRENCY.

4*s.* 6*d.*

T. Davison, Lombard-street,
Whitefriars, London.

PROPOSALS

FOR AN

ECONOMICAL AND SECURE

CURRENCY;

WITH

OBSERVATIONS

ON THE

PROFITS OF THE BANK OF ENGLAND,

AS THEY REGARD THE PUBLIC AND THE PROPRIETORS
OF BANK STOCK.

BY DAVID RICARDO, ESQ.

SECOND EDITION.

LONDON:

PRINTED FOR JOHN MURRAY, ALBEMARLE-STREET.

1816.

INTRODUCTION.

THE following important questions concerning the Bank of England will, next session, come under the discussion of parliament:

1st. Whether the Bank shall be obliged to pay their notes in specie at the demand of the holders?

2dly. Whether any alteration shall be made in the terms agreed upon in 1808, between Government and the Bank, for the management of the national debt?

And, 3dly, what compensation the public shall receive for the large amount of public deposits from which the Bank derive profit?

In point of importance, the first of these questions greatly surpasses the rest:—but so much has already been written on the subject of currency, and on the laws by which it should be regulated, that I should not trouble the reader with any further observations on those topics, did I not think that a more economical mode of effecting our payments might be advantageously adopted; to explain which, it will be necessary to premise briefly some of the general principles which are found to constitute the laws of currency, and to vindicate them from some of the objections which are brought against them.

The other two questions, though inferior in importance, are, at these times of pressure on our finances, when economy is so essential, well deserving of the serious consideration of parliament. If, on examination, it should be found that the services performed by the Bank for the public are most prodigally paid; and that this wealthy corporation has been accumulating a treasure of which no example can be brought —much of it at the expense of the public, and owing to the negligence and forbearance of government—a better arrangement, it is hoped, will now be made; which, while it secures to the Bank a just compensation for the responsibility and trouble which the management of the public business may occasion, shall also guard against any wasteful application of the public resources.

It must, I think, be allowed, that the war, which has pressed heavily on most of the classes of the community, has been attended with unlooked for benefits to the Bank; and that in proportion to the increase of the public burdens and difficulties have been the gains of that body.

The restriction on the cash payments of the Bank, which was the effect of the war, has enabled them to raise the amount of their notes in circulation from twelve millions to twenty-eight millions; whilst, at the same time, it has exonerated them from all necessity of keeping any large deposit of cash and bullion, a part of their assets from which they derive no profit.

The war too has raised the unredeemed public debt, of which the Bank have the management, from 220 to 830 millions; and notwithstanding the reduced rate of charge, they will receive for the management of the debt alone, in the present year, 277,000*l*.*, whereas in 1792 their whole receipt on acount of the debt was 99,800*l*.

It is to the war that the Bank are also indebted for the increase in the amount of public deposits. In 1792 these deposits were probably less than four millions. In and since 1806 we know that they have generally exceeded eleven millions.

It cannot, I think, be doubted, that all the ser-

* See Appendix, No. 3.

vices, which the Bank perform for the public, could be performed, by public servants and in public offices established for that purpose, at a reduction or saving of expense of nearly half a million per annum.

In 1786 the auditors of public accounts stated it as their opinion, that the public debt, then amounting to 224 millions, could be managed by government for less than 187*l*. 10*s*. per million. On a debt of 830 millions the Bank are paid 340*l*. per million on 600 millions, and 300*l*. per million on 230 millions.

Against the mode in which the public business is managed at the Bank no complaint can be justly made; ability, regularity, and precision, are to be found in every office; and in these particulars it is not probable that any change could be made which would be deemed an improvement.

As far as the public are bound to the Bank by any existing agreement, an objection, on that score, will be urged against any alteration. Inadequate as, in my opinion, was, at that time, and under the circumstances in which it was granted, the compensation which the public received from the Bank, for the renewal of their charter, I shall not plead for a revision of that contract; but permit the Bank to enjoy unmo-

lested all the fruits of so improvident and un-
equal a bargain.

But the agreement entered into with the
Bank in 1808, for the management of the national debt, is not, I think, of the above description, and either party is now at liberty to annul
it. The agreement was for no definite period;
and has no necessary connexion with the duration
of the charter, which was made eight years before
it. Applying to the state of things existing at
the time of its formation, or such a state as might
be expected to occur within a few years, it is
not any longer binding. This is declared in
the following passage of Mr. Perceval's letter
to the Bank, dated the 15th January, 1808, on
accepting the scale in respect to the rate for management proposed by the Bank. " Under this
impression," says Mr. Perceval, " I am strongly
inclined to give way to the suggestion of the
Bank in the minor parts of the arrangement,
and will therefore accede to the scale of allowances therein proposed for the management of
the public debt, *so far as it applies to present
circumstances, or to such as can be expected to
occur within any short period."* Eight years
having since elapsed, and the unredeemed debt
having, in that time, increased 280 millions, can
it be justly contended that it is not in the power

of either party, now or hereafter, to annul this agreement, or to propose such alterations in it as time and circumstances may render expedient ?

To Mr. Grenfell I am very materially indebted; I have done little more, on this part of the subject, than repeat his arguments and statements. I have endeavoured to give my feeble aid to a cause which he has already so ably advocated in parliament, and in which I trust success will crown his future efforts.

SECTION I.

In the medium of circulation—cause of uniformity is cause of goodness.

ALL writers on the subject of money have agreed that uniformity in the value of the circulating medium is an object greatly to be desired. Every improvement therefore which can promote an approximation to that object, by diminishing the causes of variation, should be adopted. No plan can possibly be devised which will maintain money at an absolutely uniform value, because it will always be subject to those variations to which the commodity itself is subject, which has been fixed upon as the standard.

While the precious metals continue to be the standard of our currency, money must necessarily undergo the same variations in value as those metals. It was the comparative steadiness in the value of the precious metals, for periods of some duration, which probably was the cause of the preference given to them in all countries, as a standard by which to measure the value of other things.

A currency may be considered as perfect, of which the standard is invariable, which always conforms to that standard, and in the use of which the utmost economy is practised.

Amongst the advantages of a paper over a metallic circulation, may be reckoned, as not the least, the facility with which it may be altered in quantity, as the wants of commerce and temporary circumstances may require : enabling the desirable object of keeping money at an uniform value to be, as far as it is otherwise practicable, securely and cheaply attained.

The quantity of metal, employed as money, in effecting the payments of any particular country, using metallic money; or the quantity of metal for which paper money is the substitute, if paper money be partly or wholly used, must depend on three things: first, on its value ;—secondly, on the amount or value of the payments to be made ;—and, thirdly, on the degree of economy practised in effecting those payments.

A country using gold as its standard would require, at least, fifteen times less of that metal

than it would of silver, if using silver, and nine
hundred times less than it would of copper, if
using that metal,—fifteen to one being about
the proportion which gold bears in value to
silver, and nine hundred to one the proportion
which it bears to copper. If the denomination
of a pound were given to any specific weight
of these metals, fifteen times more of such
pounds would be required in the one case, and
nine hundred times more in the other, whether
the metals themselves were employed as money,
or paper was partly, or entirely, substituted for
them. And if a country uniformly employed
the same metal as a standard, the quantity of
money required would be in an inverse proportion to the value of that metal. Suppose the
metal to be silver, and that, from the difficulty
of working the mines, silver should be doubled
in value,—half the quantity only would then be
wanted for money ; and if the whole business of
circulation were carried on by paper, of which
the standard was silver,—to sustain that paper,
at its bullion value, it must in like manner be
reduced one half. In the same way it might be
shewn, that, if silver became as cheap again,
compared with all other commodities, double
the quantity would be required to circulate the
same quantity of goods.—When the number of

transactions increase in any country from its increasing opulence and industry—bullion remaining at the same value, and the economy in the use of money also continuing unaltered— the value of money will rise on account of the increased use which will be made of it, and will continue permanently above the value of bullion, unless the quantity be increased, either by the addition of paper, or by procuring bullion to be coined into money. There will be more commodities bought and sold, but at lower prices; so that the same money will still be adequate to the increased number of transactions, by passing in each transaction at a higher value. The value of money then does not wholly depend upon its absolute quantity, but on its quantity relatively to the payments which it has to accomplish; and the same effects would follow from either of two causes—from increasing the uses for money one tenth—or from diminishing its quantity one tenth; for, in either case, its value would rise one tenth.

It is the rise in the value of money above the value of bullion which is always, in a sound state of the currency, the cause of its increase in quantity; for it is at these times that either an opening is made for the issue of more paper money, which is always attended with profit to the issuers; or that a profit is made by carrying bullion to the mint to be coined.

To say that money is more valuable than bullion or the standard, is to say that bullion is selling in the market under the mint price. It can therefore be purchased, coined, and issued as money, with a profit equal to the difference between the market and mint prices. The mint price of gold is 3*l*. 17*s*. 10½*d*. If, from increasing opulence, more commodities came to be bought and sold, the first effect would be that the value of money would rise. Instead of 3*l*. 17*s*. 10½*d*. of coined money being equal in value to an ounce of gold, 3*l*. 15*s*. 0*d*. might be equal to that value; and therefore a profit of 2*s*. 10½*d*. might be made on every ounce of gold that was carried to the mint to be coined. This profit, however, could not long continue; for the quantity of money which, by these means, would be added to the circulation, would sink its value, whilst the diminishing quantity of bullion in the market would also tend to raise the value of bullion to that of coin : from one or both these causes a perfect equality in their value could not fail to be soon restored.

It appears then, that, if the increase in the circulation were supplied by means of coin, the value both of bullion and money would, for a

time at least, even after they had found their
level, be higher than before; a circumstance
which though often unavoidable, is inconvenient,
as it affects all former contracts. This inconvenience is wholly got rid of, by the issue of paper
money; for, in that case, there will be no additional demand for bullion; consequently its value
will continue unaltered; and the new paper
money, as well as the old, will conform to that
value.

Besides, then, all the other advantages attending the use of paper money; by the judicious
management of the quantity, a degree of uniformity, which is by no other means attainable, is
secured to the value of the circulating medium
in which all payments are made.

The value of money and the amount of payments remaining the same, the quantity of money
required must depend on the degree of economy
practised in the use of it. If no payments were
made by checks on bankers; by means of which
money is merely written off one account and
added to another, and that to the amount of millions daily, with few or no bank notes or coin
passing; it is obvious that considerably more
currency would be required, or, which is the
same in its effects, the same money would pass
at a greatly increased value, and would therefore

be adequate to the additional amount of payments.

Whneever merchants, then, have a want of confidence in each other, which disinclines them to deal on credit, or to accept in payment each other's checks, notes, or bills ; more money, whether it be paper or metallic money, is in demand; and the advantage of a paper circulation, when established on correct principles, is, that this additional quantity can be presently supplied without occasioning any variation in the value of the whole currency, either as compared with bullion or with any other commodity ; whereas, with a system of metallic currency, this additional quantity cannot be so readily supplied, and when it is finally supplied, the whole of the currency, as well as bullion, has acquired an increased value.

SECTION II.

Use of a standard commodity—objections to it considered.

During the late discussions on the bullion question, it was most justly contended, that a cur-

rency, to be perfect, should be absolutely invariable in value.

But it was said too, that ours had become such
a currency, by the Bank restriction bill; for by
that bill we had wisely discarded gold and silver
as the standard of our money; and in fact that a
pound note did not and ought not to vary with a
given quantity of gold, more than with a given
quantity of any other commodity. This idea of
a currency without a specific standard was, I
believe, first advanced by Sir James Steuart,*
but no one has yet been able to offer any test
by which we could ascertain the uniformity in
the value of a money so constituted. Those who
supported this opinion did not see, that such a
currency, instead of being invariable, was subject to the greatest variations,—that the only use
of a standard is to regulate the quantity, and by
the quantity the value of the currency—and
that without a standard it would be exposed to
all the fluctuations to which the ignorance or the
interests of the issuers might subject it.

It has indeed been said that we might judge

* The writings of Sir James Steuart on the subject of coin
and money are full of instruction, and it appears surprising
that he could have adopted the above opinion, which is so
directly at variance with the general principles he endeavoured to establish.

of its value by its relation, not to one, but to the mass of commodities. If it should be conceded, which it cannot be, that the issuers of paper money would be willing to regulate the amount of their circulation by such a test, they would have no means of so doing; for when we consider that commodities are continually varying in value, as compared with each other; and that when such variation takes place, it is impossible to ascertain which commodity has increased, which diminished in value, it must be allowed that such a test would be of no use whatever.

Some commodities are rising in value, from the effects of taxation, from the scarcity of the raw material of which they are made, or from any other cause which increases the difficulty of production. Others again are falling, from improvements in machinery, from the better division of labour, and the improved skill of the workman; from the greater abundance of the raw material, and generally from greater facility of production. To determine the value of a currency by the test proposed, it would be necessary to compare it successively with the thousands of commodities which are circulating in the community, allowing to each all the effects which may have been produced upon its value by the above causes. To do this is evidently impossible.

To suppose that such a test would be of use in practice, arises from a misconception of the difference between price and value.

The price of a commodity is its exchangeable value in money only.

The value of a commodity is estimated by the quantity of other things generally for which it will exchange.

The price of a commodity may rise while its value falls, and *vice versa*. A hat may rise from twenty to thirty shillings in price, but thirty shillings may not procure so much tea, sugar, coffee, and all other things, as twenty shillings did before, consequently a hat cannot procure so much. The hat, then, has fallen in value, though it has increased in price.

Nothing is so easy to ascertain as a variation of price, nothing so difficult as a variation of value; indeed, without an invariable measure of value, and none such exists, it is impossible to ascertain it with any certainty or precision.

A hat may exchange for less of tea, sugar, and coffee, than before, but, at the same time, it may exchange for more of hardware, shoes, stockings, &c. and the difference of the comparative value of these commodities may either arise from a stationary value of one, and a rise, though in different degrees, of the other two; or a stationary value in one, and a fall in the value of the other two; or they may have all varied at the same time.

If we say that value should be measured by the enjoyments which the exchange of the commodity can procure for its owner, we are still as much at a loss as ever to estimate value, because two persons may derive very different degrees of enjoyment from the possession of the same commodity. In the above instance, a hat would appear to have fallen in value to him whose enjoyments consisted in tea, coffee, and sugar; while it would appear to have risen in value to him who preferred shoes, stockings, and hardware.

Commodities generally, then, can never become a standard to regulate the quantity and value of money; and although some inconveniences attend the standard which we have adopted, namely, gold and silver, from the variations to which they are subject as commodities, these are trivial, indeed, compared to those which we should have to bear, if we adopted the plan recommended.

When gold, silver, and almost all other commodities, were raised in price, during the last

c

twenty years, instead of ascribing any part of this rise to the fall of the paper currency, the supporters of an abstract currency had always some good reason at hand for the alteration in price. Gold and silver rose because they were scarce, and were in great demand to pay the immense armies which were then embodied. All other commodities rose because they were taxed either directly or indirectly, or because from a succession of bad seasons, and the difficulties of importation, corn had risen considerably in value; which, according to their theory, must necessarily raise the price of commodities. According to them, the only things which were unalterable in value were bank notes; which were, therefore, eminently well calculated to measure the value of all other things.

If the rise had been 100 per cent., it might equally have been denied that the currency had any thing to do with it, and it might equally have been ascribed to the same causes. The argument is certainly a safe one, because it cannot be disproved. When two commodities vary in relative value, it is impossible with certainty to say, whether the one rises, or the other falls; so that, if we, adopted a currency without a standard, there is no degree of depreciation to which it might not be carried. The depreciation could not admit of proof, as it might always be affirmed that commodities had risen in value, and that money had not fallen.

SECTION III.

The standard, its imperfections—Variations below without allowance of the countervailing variations above the standard, their effects—Correspondence with the standard the rule for paper money.

WHILE a standard is used, we are subject to only such a variation in the value of money, as the *standard* itself is subject to; but against such variation there is no possible remedy, and late events have proved that, during periods of war, when gold and silver are used for the payment of large armies, distant from home, those variations are much more considerable than has been generally allowed. This admission only proves that gold and silver are not so good a standard as they have been hitherto supposed ; that they are themselves subject to greater variations than it is desirable a standard should be subject to. They are, however, the best with which we are acquainted. If any other commodity, less variable, could be found, it might very properly be adopted as the future standard of our money, provided it had all the other qualities which fitted it for that purpose; but, while these metals are the standard, the currency should conform in value to them, and whenever it does not, and the market price of bullion is above the mint price, the currency is depreciated.—This proposition is unanswered, and is unanswerable.

Much inconvenience arises from using two metals as the standard of our money ; and it has long been a disputed point whether gold or silver should by law be made the principal or sole standard of money. In favour of gold, it may be said, that its greater value under a smaller bulk eminently qualifies it for the standard in an opulent country; but this very quality subjects it to greater variations of value during periods of war, or extensive commercial discredit, when it is often collected and hoarded, and may be urged as an argument against its use. The only objection to the use of silver,

as the standard, is its bulk, which renders it un-
fit for the large payments required in a wealthy
country; but this objection is entirely removed
by the substituting of paper money as the general circulation medium of the country. Silver,
too, is much more steady in its value, in consequence of its demand and supply being more
regular; and as all foreign countries regulate the
value of their money by the value of silver, there
can be no doubt, that, on the whole, silver is
preferable to gold as a standard, and should be
permanently adopted for that purpose.

A better system of currency may, perhaps,
be *imagined* than that which existed before the
late laws made bank notes a legal tender; but
while the law recognized a standard, while the
mint was open to any person, who chose, to take
thither gold and silver to be coined into money,
there was no other limit to the fall in the value
of money than to the fall in the value of the
precious metals. If gold had become as plenti-
ful and as cheap as copper, bank notes would
necessarily have partaken of the same depreciation, and all persons the whole of whose posses-
sions consisted of money—such as those who hold
exchequer bills, who discount merchants' bills,
or whose income is derived from annuities, as
the holders of the public funds, mortgagees, and

many others—would have borne all the evils of such a depreciation. With what justice, then, can it be maintained, that when gold and silver rise, money should be kept by force and by legislative interference at its former value; while no means are, or ever have been, used to prevent the fall of money when gold and silver fall? If the person possessed of money is subject to all the inconveniences of the fall in the value of his property, he ought also to have the benefits of the rise. If a paper currency without a standard be an improvement, let it be proved to be so, and then let the standard be disused; but do not preserve it to the disadvantage solely, never to the advantage, of a class of persons possessed of one out of the thousands of commodities which are circulating in the community, of which no other is subject to any such rule.

The issuers of paper money should regulate their issues solely by the price of bullion, and never by the quantity of their paper in circulation. The quantity can never be too great nor too little, while it preserves the same value as the standard. Money, indeed, should be rather *more* valuable than bullion, to compensate for the trifling delay which takes place before it i returned in exchange for bullion at the mint. This delay is equivalent to a small seignorage;

and coined money, or bank notes, which repre-
sent coined money, should, in their natural and
perfect state, be just so much more valuable
than bullion. The Bank of England, by not
having paid a due regard to this principle, have,
in former times, been considerable losers. They
supplied the country with all the coined money
for which it had occasion, and, consequently,
purchased bullion with their paper, that they
might carry it to the mint to be coined. If their
paper had been sustained, by limiting its quantity, at a value somewhat greater than bullion,
they would, in the cheapness of their purchases,
have covered all the expenses of brokerage and
refining, including the just equivalent for the
delay at the mint.

SECTION IV.

An expedient to bring the English currency as near as possible to perfection.

In the next session of parliament, the subject of currency is again to be discussed; and, probably, a time will then be fixed for the resumption of cash payments, which will oblige the Bank to limit the quantity of their paper till it conforms to the value of bullion.

A well regulated paper currency is so great an improvement in commerce, that I should greatly regret, if prejudice should induce us to return to a system of less utility. The introduction of the precious metals for the purposes of money may with truth be considered as one of the most important steps towards the improvement of commerce, and the arts of civilised life; but it is no less true that, with the advancement of knowledge and science, we discover that it would be another improvement to banish them again from the employment to which, during a less enlightened period, they had been so advantageously applied.

If the Bank should be again called upon to pay their notes in specie, the effect would be to lessen greatly the profits of the Bank without a correspondent gain to any other part of the community. If those who use one and two, and even five pounds notes, should have their option of using guineas, there can be little doubt which they would prefer; and thus, to indulge a mere caprice, a most expensive medium would be substituted for one of little value.

Besides the loss to the Bank, which must be considered as a loss to the community, general wealth being made up of individual riches, the state would be subjected to the useless expense of coinage, and, on every fall of the exchange, guineas would be melted and exported.

To secure the public against any other variations in the value of the currency than those to which the standard itself is subject, and, at the same time, to carry on the circulation with a medium the least expensive, is to attain the most perfect state to which a currency can be brought, and we should possess all these advantages by subjecting the Bank to the delivery of uncoined gold or silver at the mint standard and price, in exchange for their notes, instead of the delivery of guineas; by which means paper would never fall below the value of bullion without being followed by a reduction of its quantity. To prevent the rise of paper above the value of bullion, the Bank should be also obliged to give their paper in exchange for standard gold at the price of 3*l*. 17*s*. per ounce. Not to give too much trouble to the Bank, the quantity of gold to be demanded in exchange for paper at the mint price of 3*l*. 17*s*. 10½*d*., or the quantity to be sold to the Bank at 3*l*. 17*s*., should never be less than twenty ounces. In other words, the Bank should be obliged to purchase any quantity of gold that was offered them, not less than twenty ounces, at 3*l*. 17*s*.* per ounce, and to sell any quantity that might be demanded at 3*l*. 17*s*. 10½*d*. While

---

* The price of 3*l*. 17*s*. here mentioned, is, of course, an arbitrary price. There might be good reason, perhaps, for fixing it either a little above, or a little below. In naming 3*l*. 17*s*. I wish only to elucidate the principle. The price ought to be so fixed as to make it the interest of the seller of gold rather to sell it to the Bank than to carry it to the mint to be coined.

The same remark applies to the specified quantity of twenty ounces. There might be good reason for making it ten or thirty.

they have the power of regulating the quantity of their paper, there is no possible inconvenience that could result to them from such a regulation.

The most perfect liberty should be given, at the same time, to export or import every description of bullion. These transactions in bullion would be very few in number, if the Bank regulated their loans and issues of paper by the criterion which I have so often mentioned, namely, the price of standard bullion, without attending to the absolute quantity of paper in circulation*.

The object which I have in view would be in a great measure attained, if the Bank were obliged to deliver uncoined bullion in exchange for their notes at the mint price and standard; though they were not under the necessity of purchasing any quantity of bullion offered them at the prices to be fixed, particularly if the mint were

---

* I have already observed that silver appears to me to be best adapted for the standard of our money. If it were made so by law, the Bank should be obliged to buy or sell silver bullion only. If gold be exclusively the standard, the Bank should be required to buy or sell gold only; but if both metals be retained as the standard, as they now by law are, the Bank should have the option which of the two metals they would give in exchange for their notes, and a price should be fixed for silver rather under the standard, at which they should not be at liberty to refuse to purchase.

to continue open to the public for the coinage of money : for that regulation is merely suggested to prevent the value of money from varying from the value of bullion more than the trifling difference between the prices at which the Bank should buy and sell, and which would be an approximation to that uniformity in its value which is acknowledged to be so desirable.

If the Bank capriciously limited the quantity of their paper, they would raise its value; and gold might appear to fall below the limits at which I propose the Bank should purchase. Gold, in that case, might be carried to the mint, and the money returned from thence being added to the circulation would have the effect of lowering its value, and making it again conform to the standard; but it would neither be done so safely, so economically, nor so expeditiously, as by the means which I have proposed; against which the Bank can have no objection to offer, as it is for their interest to furnish the circulation with paper, rather than oblige others to furnish it with coin.

Under such a system, and with a currency so regulated, the Bank would never be liable to any embarrassments whatever, excepting on those extraordinary occasions, when a general panic seizes the country, and when every one is desirous of possessing the precious metals as the most convenient mode of realizing or concealing his property. Against such panics, Banks have no security, *on any system;* from their very nature they are subject to them, as at no time can there be in a Bank, or in a country, so much specie or bullion as the monied individuals of such country have a right to demand. Should every man withdraw his balance from his banker on the same day, many times the quantity of bank notes now in circulation would be insufficient to answer such a demand. A panic of this kind was the cause of the crisis in 1797 ; and not, as has been supposed, the large advances which the Bank had then made to government. Neither the Bank nor government were at that time to blame ; it was the contagion of the unfounded fears of the timid part of the community, which occasioned the run on the Bank, and it would equally have taken place if they had not made any advances to government, and had possessed twice their present capital. If the Bank had continued paying in cash, probably the panic would have subsided before their coin had been exhausted.

With the known opinion of the Bank directors, as to the rule for issuing paper money, they may be said to have exercised their powers without any great indiscretion. It is evident that they have followed their own principle with extreme caution. In the present state of the law; they have the power, without any control whatever, of increasing or reducing the circulation in any degree they may think proper: a power which should neither be intrusted to the state itself, nor to any body in it; as there can be no security for the uniformity in the value of the currency, when its augmentation or diminution depends solely on the will of the issuers. That the Bank have the power of reducing the circulation to the very narrowest limits will not be denied, even by those who agree in opinion with the directors, that they have not the power of adding indefinitely to its quantity. Though I am fully assured, that it is both against the interest and the wish of the Bank to exercise this power to the detriment of the public, yet when I contemplate the evil consequences which might ensue from a sudden and great reduction of the circulation, as well as from a great addition to it, I cannot but deprecate the facility with which the state has armed the Bank with so formidable a prerogative.

The inconvenience to which country banks were subjected before the restriction on cash payments, must at times have been very great. At all periods of alarm, or of expected alarm, they must have been under the necessity of providing themselves with guineas, that they might be prepared for every exigency which might occur. Guineas, on these occasions, were obtained at the Bank in exchange for the larger notes, and were conveyed by some confidential agent, at expense and risk, to the country bank. After performing the offices to which they were destined, they found their way again to London, and in all probability were again lodged in the Bank, provided they had not suffered such a loss of weight, as to reduce them below the legal standard.

If the plan now proposed, of paying bank notes in bullion, be adopted, it would be necessary either to extend the same privilege to country banks, or to make bank notes a legal tender, in which latter case there would be no alteration in the law respecting country banks, as they would be required, precisely as they now are, to pay their notes, when demanded, in Bank of England notes.

The saving which would take place, from not submitting the guineas to the loss of weight, from the friction which they must undergo in their repeated journeys, as well as of the expenses of conveyance, would be considerable; but by far the greatest advantage would result from the permanent supply of the country, as well as of the London circulation, as far as

the smaller payments are concerned, being provided in the very cheap medium, paper, instead
of the very valuable medium, gold; thereby
enabling the country to derive all the profit
which may be obtained by the productive employment of a capital to that amount. We
should surely not be justified in rejecting so de-
cided a benefit, unless some specific inconvenience could be pointed out as likely to follow
from adopting the cheaper medium.

Much has been ably written on the benefits
resulting to a country from the liberty of trade,
leaving every man to employ his talents, and
capital, as to him may seem best, unshackled
by restrictions of every kind. The reasoning
by which the liberty of trade is supported, is
so powerful, that it is daily obtaining converts.
It is with pleasure, that I see the progress
which this great principle is making amongst
those whom we should have expected to cling
the longest to old prejudices. In the petitions
to parliament against the corn bill, the advantages of an unrestricted trade were generally recognised; but by none more ably than by the
clothiers of Gloucestershire, who were so convinced of the impolicy of restriction, that they
expressed a willingness to relinquish every
restraint which might be found to attach to

their trade. These are principles which cannot be too widely extended, nor too generally adopted in practice; but if foreign nations are not sufficiently enlightened to adopt this liberal system, and should continue their prohibitions and excessive duties on the importation of our commodities and manufactures, let England set them a good example by benefiting herself; and instead of meeting their prohibitions by similar exclusions, let her get rid, as soon as she can, of every vestige of so absurd and hurtful a policy.

The pecuniary advantage which would be the result of such a system would soon incline other states to adopt the same course, and no long period would elapse before the general prosperity would be seen to be best promoted by each country falling naturally into the most advantageous employment of its capital, talents, and industry.

Advantageous, however, as the liberty of trade would prove, it must be admitted that there are a few, and a very few exceptions to it, where the interference of government may be beneficially exerted. Monsieur Say, in his able work on Political Economy, after shewing the advantages of a free trade, observes *, that the

* Economie Politique, livre i. chap. 17.

D

interference of government is justifiable only in two cases; first, to prevent a fraud, and secondly, to certify a fact. In the examinations to which medical practitioners are obliged to submit, there is no improper interference; for it is necessary to the welfare of the people, that the fact of their having acquired a certain portion of knowledge respecting the diseases of the human frame should be ascertained and certified. The same may be said of the stamp which government puts on plate and money; it thereby prevents fraud, and saves the necessity of having recourse on each purchase and sale to a difficult chemical process. In examining the purity of drugs sold by chemists and apothecaries, the same object is had in view. In all these cases, the purchasers are not supposed to have, or to be able to acquire sufficient knowledge to guard them against deception; and government interferes to do that for them which they could not do for themselves.

But if the public require protection against the inferior money which might be imposed upon them by an undue mixture of alloy, and which is obtained by means of the government stamp when metallic money is used; how much more necessary is such protection when paper money forms the whole, or almost the whole, of the circulating medium of the country? Is it not inconsistent, that government should use its power to protect the community from the loss of one shilling in a guinea; but does not interfere to protect them from the loss of the whole twenty shillings in a one pound note? In the case of Bank of England notes, a guarantee is taken by the government for the notes which the Bank issue; and the whole capital of the Bank, amounting to more than eleven millions and a half, must be lost before the holders of their notes can be sufferers from any imprudence they may commit. Why is not the same principle followed with respect to the country banks? What objection can there be against requiring of those who take upon themselves the office of furnishing the public with a circulating medium, to deposit with government an adequate security for the due performance of their engagements? In the use of money, every one is a trader; those whose habits and pursuits are little suited to explore the mechanism of trade are obliged to make use of money, and are no way qualified to ascertain the solidity of the different banks whose paper is in circulation; accordingly we find that men living on limited incomes, women, labourers, and mechanics of all descriptions, are often severe sufferers by the failures of country banks, which have lately become frequent beyond all former example. Though I am by no means disposed to judge uncharitably of those who have occasioned so much ruin and distress to the middle and lower classes of the people, yet, it must be allowed by the most indulgent, that the true business of banking must be very much abused before it can be necessary for any bank, possessing the most moderate funds, to fail in their engagements; and I believe it will be found, in by far the major part of these failures, that the parties can be charged with offences much more grave than those of mere imprudence and want of caution.

Against this inconvenience the public should be protected by requiring of every country bank to deposit with government, or with commissioners appointed for that purpose, funded property or other government security, in some proportion to the amount of their issues.

Into the details of such a plan it is not necessary to enter very minutely. Stamps for the issue of notes might be delivered on the required deposit being made, and certain periods in the year might be fixed upon, when the whole or any part of the security should be returned, on proof being given, either by the return of the cancelled stamps, or by any other satisfactory means, that the notes for which it was given were no longer in circulation.

Against such a regulation no country bank of respectability would object; on the contrary, it would, in all probability, be most acceptable to them, as it would prevent the competition of those, who are at present so little entitled to appear in the market against them.

SECTION V.

A practice which creates a great mass of mercantile inconvenience—Remedy proposed.

AFTER all the improvements however that can be made in our system of currency, there will yet be a temporary inconvenience, to which the public will be subject, as they have hitherto been, from the large quarterly payment of dividends to the public creditors;—an inconvenience which is often severely felt; and to which I think an easy remedy might be applied.

The national debt has become so large, and the interest which is paid quarterly upon it is

so great a sum, that the mere collecting the
money from the receivers general of the taxes,
and the consequent reduction of the quantity in
circulation, just previously to its being paid to
the public creditor, in *January, April, July,* and
October, occasions, for a week or more, the most
distressing want of circulating medium. The
Bank, by judicious management, discounting
bills probably very freely, just at the time that
these monies are paid into the Exchequer, and
arranging for the receipt of large sums, immediately after the payment of the dividends, have,
no doubt, considerably lessened the inconvenience to the mercantile part of the community.
Nevertheless, it is well known to those who are
acquainted with the money market that the distress for money is extreme at the periods I have
mentioned. Exchequer bills, which usually sell
at a premium of five shillings per 100*l.* are at such
times at so great a discount, that by the purchase
of them then, and the re-sale when the dividends
are paid, a profit may often be made equal to
the rate of fifteen to twenty per cent. interest
for money. At these times, too, the difference
between the price of stock for ready money,
and the price for a week or two to come, affords
a profit, to those who can advance money, even
greater than can be made by employing mo-

ney in the purchase of exchequer bills. This great distress for money is frequently, after the dividends are paid, followed by as great a plenty, so that little use can for some time be made of it.

The very great perfection to which our system of economizing the use of money has arrived, by the various operations of banking, rather aggravates the peculiar evil of which I am speaking; because, when the quantity of circulation is reduced, in consequence of the improvements which have been adopted in the means of effecting our payments, the abstraction of a million or two from that reduced circulation becomes much more serious in its effects, being so much larger a proportion of the whole circulation.

On the inconvenience to which trade and commerce are exposed by this periodical distress for money, I should think no difference of opinion can possibly exist. The same unanimity may not prevail with respect to the remedy which I shall now propose.

Let the Bank be authorised by government to deliver the dividend warrants to the proprietors of stock a few days *before* the receivers-general are required to pay their balances into the Exchequer.

Let these warrants be payable to the bearer exactly in the same manner as they now are.

Let the day for the payment of these dividend warrants in bank notes be regulated precisely as it now is.

If the day of payment could be named on or before the delivery of the warrants, it would be more convenient.

Finally, let these warrants be receivable into the Exchequer from the receivers general, or from any other person who may have payments to make there, in the same manner as bank notes; the persons paying them allowing the discount for the number of days which will elapse before they become due.

If a plan of this sort were adopted there could never be any particular scarcity of money before the payment of the dividends, nor any particular plenty of it after. The quantity of money in circulation would be neither increased nor diminished by the payment of the dividends. A great part of these warrants would, from the stimulus of private interest, infallibly find their way into the hands of those who had public payments to make, and from them to the Exchequer. Thus then would a great part of the payments to government, and the payments from government to the public creditor, be effected without the intervention of either bank notes or money; and the demands for money for such purposes, which are now so severely felt by the mercantile classes, would be effectually prevented.

Those who are well acquainted with the economical system, now adopted in London, throughout the whole banking concern, will readily understand that the plan here proposed is merely the extension of this economical system to a species of payments to which it has not yet been applied. To them it will be unnecessary to say any thing further in recommendation of a plan, with the advantages of which, in other concerns, they are already so familiar.

SECTION VI.

The public services of the Bank excessively over-paid—Remedy proposed.

Mr. Grenfell has lately called the attention of parliament to a subject of importance to the financial interests of the community. At a time when taxes bear so heavy on the people, brought upon them by the unexampled difficulties and expenses of the war, a resource so obvious as that which he has pointed out will surely not be neglected.

It appears by the documents which Mr. Grenfell's motions have produced, that the Bank have, for many years, on an average, had no less a sum of the public money in their hands, on which they have obtained an interest of five per cent., than eleven millions; and the only compensation which the public have derived for the advantage which the Bank have so long enjoyed is a loan of three millions from 1806 to 1814, a period of eight years, at an interest of three per cent.—and a further loan of three millions, without interest, which the Bank, in 1808, agreed to afford the public till six months after the definitive treaty of peace, and which by an act of last session was continued without interest till April 1816. From 1806 to 1816, a period of ten years, the Bank have gained five per cent. per annum on 11,000,000*l.*, which will amount to £5,500,000

During the same time the public have received the following compensation: the difference between three per cent. and five per cent. interest; or, two per cent. per annum on 3,000,000*l.* for eight years, or - - - £480,000

From 1808 to 1816, the public will have had the advantage of a loan of three millions without interest, which at five per cent. per ann. would amount, in eight years, to £1,200,000
————— 1,680,000

Balance gained by the Bank - - - 3,820,000

3,820,000*l.* will have been gained by the Bank in ten years, or 382,000*l.* per ann. for acting as bankers to the public, when, perhaps, the whole expense attending this department of their business does not exceed 10,000*l.* per ann.

In 1807, when these advantages were first noticed by a committee of the house of commons, it was contended, by many persons, in favour of the Bank, and by Mr. Thornton, one of the directors who had been governor, that the gains of the Bank were in proportion to the amount of their notes in circulation, and that no advantage was derived from the public deposits, further than as they enabled the Bank to maintain a larger amount of notes in circulation. This fallacy was completely exposed by the committee.

If Mr. Thornton's argument were correct, no advantage whatever would have resulted to the Bank from the deposits of the public money—for those deposits do not enable them to maintain a larger amount of notes in circulation.

Suppose that before the Bank had any of the public deposits, the amount of their notes in circulation were twenty-five millions, and that they derived a profit by such circulation. Suppose now that government received ten millions for taxes in bank notes, and deposited them permanently with the Bank. The circulation

would be immediately reduced to fifteen millions, but the profits of the Bank would be precisely the same as before; though fifteen millions
only were then in circulation, the Bank would
obtain a profit on twenty-five millions. If now
they again raise the circulation to twenty-five
millions, by employing the ten millions in discounting bills, purchasing exchequer bills, or
advancing the payments on the loan for the
year, for the holders of scrip receipts, will they
not have added the interest of ten millions to
their usual profits, although they should at no
time have raised their circulation above the
original sum of twenty-five millions?

That the increase in the amount of public
deposits should enable the Bank to add to the
amount of their notes in circulation is neither
supported by theory nor experience. If we attend to the progress of these deposits, we shall
observe that at no time did they increase so much
as from 1800 to 1806, during which time there
was no increase in the circulation of notes of
five pounds and upwards; but from 1807 to 1815,
when there was no increase whatever in the
amount of public deposits, the amount of notes
of five pounds and upwards had increased five
millions.

Nothing can be more satisfactory on the subject of the profits of the Bank, from the public deposits, than the report of the committee on public expenditure, in 1807. It is as follows :

" In the evidence upon this part of the sub-
" ject, it is admitted that the notes of the Bank
" are productive of profit, but it appears to be
" assumed that the government balances are
" only so in proportion as they tend to aug-
" ment the amount of notes; whereas your
" committee are fully persuaded that both ba-
" lances and notes are and must necessarily be
" productive.

" The funds of the Bank, which are the sources
" of profit, and which constitute the measure of
" the sum which they have to lend (subject only
" to a deduction on account of cash and bullion),
" may be classed under three heads.

" First. The sum received from their pro-
" prietors as capital, together with the savings
" which have been added to it.

" Secondly. The sum received from persons
" keeping cash at the Bank. This sum consists
" of the balances of the deposit accounts, both
" of government and of individuals. In 1797,
" this fund, including all the balances of indivi-

" duals, was only 5,130,140*l*. The present go-
" vernment balances alone have been stated
" already at between eleven and twelve millions,
" including bank notes deposited in the Exche-
" quer *.

" Thirdly. The sum received in return for
" notes put into circulation   A correspondent
" value for every note must originally have been
" given, and the value thus given for notes consti-
" tutes one part of the general fund to be lent
" at interest.   A note-holder, indeed, does not
" differ essentially from a person to whom a
" balance is due.   Both are creditors of the
" Bank; the one holding a note, which is the evi-
" dence of the debt due to him, the other having
" the evidence of an entry in the ledger of the
" Bank.   *The sum at all times running at inte-*
" *rest will be in exact proportion to the amount*

---

* By some of my readers the words " including bank
" notes deposited in the Exchequer" may not be understood.
They are bank notes never put into circulation; neither
are they included in any return made by the Bank.   They
are called at the Exchequer special notes, and are mere
vouchers, (not having even the form of bank notes), of the
payment to the Bank from the Exchequer of such monies as
are daily received at the latter office.   They are the record,
therefore, of a part of the public deposits lodged with the
Bank.

" *of these three funds combined, deduction being.*
" *made for the value of cash and bullion* *."

Every word of this statement appears to me
unanswerable, and the principle laid down by
the committee would afford us an infallible clue
to ascertain the net profits of the Bank, if we
knew the amount of their savings,—their cash
and bullion, and their annual expenses, as well
as the other particulars, are known to us.

It will be seen by the above extract, that in
1807 the amount of the public deposits was between eleven and twelve millions, whereas in
1797 the amount of public and private deposits
were together only equal to 5,130,140*l*. In consequence of this report, Mr. Perceval applied to
the Bank, on the part of the public, for a participation in their additional profits from this
source, either in the way of an annual payment

---

* In 1797 the Bank stated their finances to be as follows:

Bank notes in circulation	£8,640,000
Public and private deposits	5,130,140
Surplus capital	3,826,890
	17,597,030

On the other side of the account they shewed in what securities these funds were invested, and, with the exception of
cash and bullion, and a small sum for stamps, they were all
yielding interest and profit to the Bank.

or as a loan of money without interest; and, after some negociation, a loan of three millions was obtained without interest, payable six months after a definitive treaty of peace.

The same report also notices the exorbitant allowance which was made to the Bank for the management of the national debt. The public paid the Bank at that time at the rate of 450*l.* per million, for management, and it was stated by the committee that the additional allowance for management in the ten years, ending in 1807, in consequence of the increase of the debt, was more than 155,000*l.* whilst the " whole increase " of the officers who actually transact the busi- " ness, in the last eleven years, is only one hun- " dred and thirty-seven, whose annual expence " may be from 18,449*l.* to 23,290*l.*; the addition " to the other permanent charges being proba- " bly about one half or two thirds of that sum."

After this report a new agreement was made with the Bank for the management of the public debt.

450*l.* per million was to be paid if the unre-deemed capital exceeded three hundred millions, but fell below four hundred millions.

340*l.* per million, if the capital exceeded four hundred millions, but fell below six hundred millions.

300*l.* per million on such part of the public debt as exceeded six hundred millions.

Besides these allowances the Bank are paid 800*l.* per million for receiving contributions on loans; 1000*l.* on each contract for lotteries, and 1250*l.* per million, or one eighth per cent. for receiving contributions on the profits arising from property, professions, and trades. This agreement has been in force ever since.

As the period is now approaching when the affairs of the Bank will undergo the consideration of parliament, and when the agreement which regards the public deposits will expire, by the payment of the three millions borrowed of the Bank without interest, in 1808; no time can be more proper than the present to point out the undue advantages which were given to the Bank in the terms settled between them and Mr. Perceval in 1808. This I apprehend was the chief object of Mr. Grenfell; for it is not alone to the additional advantages which the Bank have obtained since the agreement in 1808 that he wishes to call the attention of parliament; but also to that agreement itself, under which the public are now paying, and have long paid, in one shape or another, enormous sums for very inadequate services.

Mr. Grenfell probably thinks, and, if he does,

I most heartily concur with him, that a profit of
382,000*l.* per annum, which is the sum at which
the advantages of the public deposits to the
Bank, for a period of ten years, may be calculated, as will be seen page 44, very far exceeds the
just compensation which the public ought to
pay to the Bank, for doing the mere business of
bankers; particularly when, in addition to this
sum, 300,000*l.* per annum is now also paid for
the management of the national debt, loans, &c.;
when moreover the Bank have been enjoying,
ever since the renewal of their charter, immense
additional profits, from the substitution of paper
money in lieu of a currency consisting partly of
metallic and partly of paper money, which additional profits were not in contemplation, either
of parliament which granted, or of the Bank
which obtained that charter, when the bargain
was made in 1800; and of which they might be
in a great measure deprived by the repeal of the
bill which restricts them from paying their notes
in specie. Under these circumstances it must, I
think, be allowed that in 1808 Mr. Perceval by
no means obtained for the public what they had
a right to expect; and it is to be hoped that,
with the known sentiments of the Chancellor of
the Exchequer, as to the right of the public to

participate in the additional advantages of the Bank, arising from public deposits, terms more consonant with the public interest will now be insisted on.

It is true that the above sums, though paid by the public, are not the net profits of the Bank; from them a deduction must be made for the expences of that part of the Bank establishment which is exclusively appropriated to the public business; but those expences do not probably exceed 150,000*l*. per annum.

The committee on public expenditure stated in their report to the House of Commons, in 1807, " that the number of clerks employed by " the Bank exclusively or principally in the " public business was,

In 1786	243
1796	313
1807	450

" whose salaries, it is presumed, may be calcu-
" lated at an average of between 120*l*. and 170*l*.
" for each clerk: taking them at 135*l*. which ex-
" ceeds the average of those employed in the
" South Sea House, the sum is - - 60,750*l*.
" at 150*l*. the sum is - - - - - 67,500*l*.
" at 170*l*. the sum is - - - - - 76,500*l*.
" either of which two last sums would be suffi-
" cient to provide a superannuation fund.

" The very moderate salaries, the report con-
" tinues, received by the governor, deputy go-
" vernor, and directors, amount to   £8,000
" Incidental expences may be es-
   " timated at about   -   -   15,000
" Building additional and repairs,
   " at about   -   -   -   10,000
" Law expences and loss by frauds,
   " forgeries, at about   -   -   10,000

                                      43,000
Add the largest estimate for clerks   76,500

                  Total   £119,500

Allowing, then, the very highest computation
of the committee, the expence of managing the
public business in 1807, including the *whole* of
the salaries of the directors, incidental expences,
additional buildings and repairs, together with
law expences and loss by frauds and forgeries,
amounted to 119,500*l.*

The committee also stated that the increased
expences of the Bank for managing the public
business, after a period of eleven years, from
1796 to 1807, were about 35,000*l.* per annum,
on an increased debt of two hundred and seventy
eight millions, being at the rate of 126*l.* per mil-

lion. From 1807 to the present time the unredeemed debt managed by the Bank has increased
from about five hundred and fifty millions to
about eight hundred and thirty millions, or
about two hundred and eighty millions—little
more than from 1796 to 1807, and therefore at
the same rate of 126*l.* per million, would be attended with a similar expence of 35,000*l.*; but,
" as the rate of expence diminishes as the scale
" of business enlarges," I shall estimate it at
30,500*l.* which added to 119,500*l.*, the expences
of 1807, will make the whole expence of managing the public business amount to 150,000*l.*
The auditors of public accounts in 1786 estimated that 187*l.* 10*s.* per million was sufficient
to pay the expences of managing a debt of two
hundred and twenty-four millions. The estimate which I have just made is about 180*l.* per
million, on a debt of eight hundred and thirty
millions, which will appear an ample allowance
when it is considered in what different propor-
ions the debt itself increases, compared with the
work which it occasions.

Supposing, then, the expences to be about
150,000*l.* the net profits obtained by the Bank
by all its transactions with the public this year
will be as follows :

Charge for managing the national
debt for one year, ending the
1st *February*, 1816*,   -   -   254,000
For receiving contributions on
loans, at 800*l.* per million, on
thirty-six millions   -   -   28,800
Ditto lotteries   -   -   2,000
Average profits on public depo-
sits†   -   -   -   382,000
Allowance for receiving property
tax   -   -   -   3,480
                                          ————
                                          670,280
Expences attending the manage-
ment of the public business   -   150,000
                                          ————
Net profits of the Bank paid by
the public   -   -   -   £520,280
                                          ————

Of this vast sum, 372,000*l.* probably aris es
from the deposits alone, an expence which might
almost wholly be saved to the nation, if government were to take the management of that concern into their own hands, by having a common

———————

* This charge is calculated on the debt as it stood in
February, 1815 : more than seventy-five millions have been
added since. See Appendix.
† See page 44.

treasury, on which each department should draw in the same manner as they now do on the Bank of England, investing the eleven millions, which appears to be the average deposits, in Exchequer bills, a part of which might be sold in the market, if any unforeseen circumstances should reduce the deposits below that sum,

The resolutions* proposed by Mr, Grenfell, and on which parliament will decide the next session, after briefly recapitulating the facts contained in the documents which his motions have produced, conclude thus: " That this House " will take into early consideration the advan- " tages derived by the Bank, as well from the " management of the national debt, as from the " amount of balances of public money remaining " in their hands, with the view to the adoption " of such an arrangement, when the engage- " ments now subsisting shall have expired, as " may be consistent with what is due to the in- " terest of the public, and the rights, credit, and " stability of the Bank of England."

Mr. Mellish, the governor of the Bank, has also proposed resolutions to be submitted to parliament next session. These resolutions* admit all the facts stated by Mr. Grenfell's; they men-

* See Appendix.

tion also one or two trifling services which the
Bank perform for the public, one without charge,*
and another at a less charge than is incurred by
employing the ordinary collector of taxes, But
the 8th and 9th resolutions advance an extraordinary pretension,—they appear to question
whether *on the expiration of the loan of 3,000,000l.*

---

* The one without charge is the calculating the deduction
from each dividend warrant for property tax.

The other is receiving contributions from those who pay
their property tax into the Bank, for which the Bank receives
1250l. per million, or one-eighth per cent.

If the collector had gone from house to house to receive
this money, he would have had an allowance of five pence
per pound, which would have cost the public 58,007l. instead of 3480l. paid to the Bank.

Perhaps no part of the business of the Bank is more easily
transacted than this which they have pointed out. Instead
of being under-paid, it appears to me to be paid most li-
berally.

The saving to the public is really effected by the money
being brought to one focus, instead of being collected from
various quarters. The Bank appear to consider the rule, by
which they are to measure the moderation of their charges,
to be the saving which they effect to their employer, rather
than the just compensation for their own trouble and expence.
What would they think of an engineer, if in his charge for
the construction of a steam engine he should be guided by
the value of the labour which the engine was calculated to
save, and not by the value of the labour and materials necessary to its construction?

in 1816, government will be at liberty before 1833, the time when the charter will expire, to demand any compensation whatever from the Bank for the advantages they derive from the public deposits, or to make any new arrangement respecting the charge for management of the national debt. These resolutions are as follows:

8th. " That by the 39 and 40 *Geo. 3. c.* 28. *s.* " 13, it is enacted," That during the continuance " of the charter, the Bank shall enjoy all privi- " leges, profits, emoluments, benefits, and ad- " vantages whatsoever, which they now possess " and enjoy by virtue of any employment by or " on behalf of the public.

" That previously to such renewal of their " charter, the Bank was employed as the public " banker, in keeping the cash of all the principal " departments in the receipt of the public re- " venue, and in issuing and conducting the pub- " lic expenditure, &c."

9th. " That whenever the engagements now " subsisting between the public and the Bank " shall expire, it may be proper to consider the " advantages derived by the Bank from its " transactions with the public, with a view to " the adoption of such arrangements as may be

" consistent with those principles of equity and
" good faith, which ought to prevail in all trans-
" actions between the public and the Bank of
" England." *

* Since the first edition of this work was published, the
first Lord of the Treasury, and the Chancellor of the Exchequer, have proposed to the Bank that they shall continue
the advance of three millions, which would have been due in
April next, for two years without interest :—and further
that the Bank shall advance the sum of six millions at four
per cent. for two years certain, and shall continue the same
for three years longer from such period, subject to repayment
upon six months notice to be given, at any time between the
10th October in any year, and the 5th of April following,
either by the Lords of the Treasury to the Bank, or by the
Bank to their Lordships. This proposal was agreed to by a
General Court of Proprietors of Bank Stock, held, on the
8th of February, for the purpose of considering the same.

At this general court, on asking for some explanation respecting the deposit of the public money at the end of the
two years, I noticed with approbation the departure of the
Bank from the claim which they had set up in the above resolutions, in which they appeared to me to assert the *right* of the
Bank to the custody of the public money without paying any
remuneration whatever; to which the Governor of the Bank,
Mr. Mellish, replied, that I had totally misconceived the
meaning of those resolutions, and he was sure if I read them
again with attention, I should be convinced that no such construction could be put on them. I am glad the Bank dis-
claim having had the intention of depriving the public of
the advantage which they have enjoyed since the report of

That the Bank should now *for the first time*
intimate that their charter precludes the public
from making any demand on the Bank for a
participation in the advantages arising from the
public deposits, after all that has passed since
1800 on that subject, does indeed appear surprising.

The charter of the Bank was renewed in 1800
for twenty-one years, from its expiration in
1812; consequently it will not now terminate
till 1833. But since 1800, so far from the Bank
asserting any such claim of right to the whole
advantages of the public deposits, they in 1806
lent government 3,000,000*l.* till 1814, at 3 per
cent. interest, and in 1808 they lent 3,000,000*l.*
more till the termination of the war, without
interest, and in the last session of parliament
the loan of 3,000,000*l.* was continued without
interest till *April* 1816. These loans were expressly granted, in consideration of the increase
in the amount of the public deposits.

the Committee on Public Expenditure ; though I regret, that
they have expressed themselves so obscurely, as to have given
me and many others a different impression. The resolutions
still appear to me to assert that the privilege of being public banker was for a valuable consideration secured to the
Bank during the continuance of their charter, and that at
the expiration of that engagement, and not before, it might
be proper to consider of a new arrangement.

The committee on public expenditure, in their report (1807), to which I have already referred, speaking of the loan of 3,000,000*l.* to the public in 1806, at three per cent. interest, observe, " But the transaction is most material in an " other view, as it evinces that the agreement " made in 1800 was not considered either by " those who acted on the part of the public, " or by the Bank directors themselves, as a bar " against further participation, whenever the in " crease of their profits derived from the public, " and the circumstances of public affairs, might, " upon similar principles, *make such a claim* " *reasonable and expedient.*" And what is Mr. Perceval's language at the same period, when in consequence of this report he applied for and obtained a loan of 3,000,000*l.* till the end of the war? In his letter to the governor and deputy governor of the Bank, dated the 11th of *January* 1808, he says, " I think it necessary to " observe, that the proposal to confine the dura " tion of the advance, by way of loan, or of the " annual payment into the Exchequer, to the " period of the present war, and twelve months " after the termination of it, is by no means to " be understood as an admission on my part, " that at the expiration of such period, the pub " lic will no longer be entitled to look to any ad-

" vantage from the continuance of such deposits,
" but simply as a provision, by which the govern-
" ment and the Bank may be respectively en-
" abled, under the change in the state of affairs
" which will then have taken place, probably
" affecting the amount of public balances in the
" hands of the latter, to consider of a new ar-
" rangement." On the 19th of *January*, Mr.
Perceval's proposals were submitted to the Court
of Directors in a more official form,—they conclude thus : " And it is understood that *during*
" *the continuance of this advance by the Bank*,
" no alteration is to be proposed in the general
" course of business, between the Bank and the
" Exchequer, nor any regulation introduced by
" which the accounts now by law directed to
" be kept at the Bank shall be withdrawn from
" thence." These proposals were recommended
for acceptance by the Court of Directors to the
Court of Proprietors, and were, without comment, agreed to on the 21st of *January*.

Mr. Vansittart, in his application to the Bank
in *November* 1814, relative to continuing the loan
of 3,000,000*l*., which would have become due on
the 17th of *December* following, till *April* 1816,
uses these words: " But I beg to be distinctly
" understood as not departing from the reserva-
" tion made by the late Mr. Perceval, in his

" letter to the governor and deputy governor of
" the Bank, of the 11th *January*, 1808, by which
" he guarded against the possibility of any mis-
" construction which could preclude the public,
" after the expiration of the period of the loan
" then agreed upon, from asserting its title to
" future advantage from the continuance or in-
" crease of such deposits; and as adhering ge-
" nerally to the principles maintained by Mr.
" Perceval, in the discussion which then took
" place."

No comment whatever appears to have been
made by the Bank on these observations: a general Court of Proprietors was called, and the
loan of three millions was continued till *April*,
1816.

It surely will not come with a very good grace
now from the Bank, to insist that the agreement
of 1800 precludes the public from demanding
any compensation for the advantages which the
Bank have derived from the increase of the public deposits since that period, when, on so many
occasions, the right of participation has been so
expressly claimed on the part of government,
and acceded to by the Court of Directors.

In addition to these strong facts, by a reference to the basis on which the agreement for the renewal of the charter was founded, as detailed by Mr. Thornton in his evidence before the committee of public expenditure in 1807*, it will still further appear, that the Bank have no claim whatever to shelter themselves under their charter, in refusing to let the public participate in the profits which have accrued from the augmentation of the public deposits.

It must be recollected that Mr. Thornton was, in 1800, the governor of the Bank; that he was the negociator, on the part of the Bank, with Mr. Pitt, for the renewal of the charter; and that, in fact, the idea of renewing the charter, so long before its expiration, originated with him. Mr. Thornton told the committee, that the only sums of public money, on which the Bank derived profit, and which were referred to by him and Mr. Pitt, with a view to settle the compensation which the public should receive for prolonging the exclusive privileges of the Bank, were those lodged at the Bank for the payment of the growing dividends, and for the quarterly issues to the commissioners for the redemption of the national debt.

* Report, page 104.

The first of these sums Mr. Thornton esti
mates to be on an average   -   £2,500,000*
And it appears by an account
  lately produced, that the second
  amounted to   615,842

$$\overline{\hspace{3cm}}$$

£3,115,842

$$\overline{\hspace{3cm}}$$

Mr. Thornton expressly states, that all other
public accounts were of trifling amount, and
" the probable augmentation of the balances
" of public money from the various departments
" of government was not taken into the ac-
" count;" " that such augmentation was neither
" adverted to, nor provided for."

If, then, it is acknowledged by the very
negociator on the part of the Bank that the
probable augmentation of the public balances
formed no part of the consideration in settling
the pecuniary remuneration which was given to
the public for continuing to the Bank their exclusive privileges, how can it now, with any
justice, be contended by the Bank, that the profits derived from those augmented balances,

* By an account laid before parliament last session, it
appears, that the amount of exchequer bills and bank notes
deposited with the Exchequer, as cash, amounted, on an
average of the year ending *March*, 1800, to 3,690,000*l.*

which were "neither adverted to, nor provided "for," belong of right exclusively to the Bank, and that the public have no claim either to participate in them, or to withdraw the balances to any use to which they may think proper to apply them.

It is to be observed, that Mr. Thornton, in his evidence before alluded to, represented all the other public accounts, excepting the two before mentioned, as of trifling amount; but, by accounts which were last session presented to parliament, it appears that in 1800, the year to which Mr. Thornton's evidence refers, when the charter was renewed, the public balances of all descriptions deposited with the Bank amounted to 6,200,000*l.*, exceeding the aggregate amount stated by Mr. Thornton, by three millions, which he would, if he had been aware of this fact, hardly have called "a trifling "amount."

If, then, the fact of this large additional deposit did not come under the consideration of Mr. Thornton and Mr. Pitt, at the time of renewing the charter; if no part of the remuneration which the public then received was founded on this fact; the large amount of public deposits in 1800, so far from entitling the Bank to retain the whole profits arising from the still larger deposits at the present period, binds them in justice to be particularly liberal in any new engagement they may now make with the public, as affording a remuneration for a profit so long enjoyed, which, it is to be presumed, they would not have been allowed to enjoy, if the facts had been clearly known and considered, at the time of settling the terms on which the charter was renewed.

But whether known or not known, must have been of little consequence in Mr. Thornton's estimation; whose opinion, that the profits of the Bank were not increased by the augmentation of the public balances, otherwise than as they contributed to increase the amount of bank notes in circulation, is so emphatically given.

Is it not lamentable to view a great and opulent body like the Bank of England, exhibiting a wish to augment their hoards by undue gains wrested from the hands of an overburthened people? Ought it not rather to have been expected that gratitude for their charter, and the unlooked for advantages with which it has been attended; for the bonuses and increased dividends which they have already shared, and for the great undivided treasure which it has further enabled them to accumulate, would have induced the Bank voluntarily to relinquish to the state, the whole benefit which is derived from the employment of eleven millions of the public money, instead of manifesting a wish to deprive them of the small portion of it which they have for a few years enjoyed?

When the rate of charge for the management of the national debt was under discussion, in 1807, Mr. Thornton said, "that in a matter between the public and the Bank, he was sure nothing but a fair compensation for trouble, risk, and actual losses, and the great responsibility that attaches to the office, would be required."

How comes it that the language of the directors of the present day is so much changed? Instead of expecting only a fair compensation for trouble, risk, and actual losses, they endeavour to deprive the public even of the inadequate compensation which they have hitherto received; and appeal, now for the first time, to their charter, for their right to hold the public money, and to enjoy all the profit which can be derived from its use, without allowing the least remuneration to the public.

If the charter were as binding as the Bank contend for, a great public company, possessing so advantageous a monopoly, and so intimately connected with the state, might be expected to act on a more liberal policy towards its generous benefactors.

Till the last session of parliament, the Bank were also particularly favoured in the composition which they paid for stamp duties. In 1791, they paid a composition of 12,000*l.* per annum, in lieu of all stamps either on bills or notes. In 1799, on an increase of the stamp duty, this composition was advanced to 20,000*l.*; and an addition of 4,000*l.*, raising the whole to 24,000*l.*, was made for the duty on notes under 5*l.*, which the Bank had then begun to circulate. In 1804, an addition of not less than 50 per cent. was made to the stamp duty imposed by the act of 1799, on notes under 5*l.*, and a considerable increase on the notes of a higher value; and although the Bank circulation of notes under 5*l.* had increased from one and a half to four and a half millions, and the amount of notes of a higher description had also increased, yet the whole composition of the Bank was only raised from 24,000*l.* to 32,000*l.* In 1808, there was a further increase of 33 per cent. to the stamp duty, at which time the composition was raised from 32,000*l.* to 42,000*l.* In both these instances the increase was not in proportion even to the increase of duty; and no allowance whatever was made for the increase in the amount of the Bank circulation.

In the last session of parliament, on a further increase of the stamp duty, the principle was for the first time established, that the Bank should pay a composition, in some proportion to the amount of their circulation. It is now fixed as follows. Upon the average circulation of the three preceding years, the Bank is to pay at the rate of 3500*l.* per million, without reference to the classes or value of the notes of which the aggregate circulation may consist.

The average of the Bank circulation for three years, ending 5th *April,* 1815, was 25,102,600*l.*; and upon this average they will pay this year about 87,500*l.*

Next year the average will be taken upon the three years, ending in *April* 1816; and if it differs from the last, the duty will vary accordingly.

If the same course had been followed now, as in 1804 and 1808, the Bank would have had to pay, even with the additional duty, only 52,500*l.,* so that 35,000*l.* per annum has been saved to the public, by parliament having at last recognized the principle which should have been adopted in 1799; and by the neglect of which, the public have probably been losers and the Bank consequently gainers, of a sum little less than 500,000*l.*

SECTION.VII.

Bank Profits and Savings—Misapplication— Proposed Remedy.

I HAVE hitherto been considering the profits of the Bank, as they regard the public, and have endeavoured to shew that they have greatly exceeded what a just consideration for *their* rights and interests could warrant.—I propose now to consider them in relation to the interests of the proprietors of Bank stock, for which purpose I shall endeavour to state a basis on which the profits of the Bank may be calculated, with a view to ascertain what the accumulated savings of the Bank now are.—If we knew accurately the expences of the Bank, and the amount of cash and bullion which they may at different times have had in their hands, we should have the means of making a calculation on this subject, which would be a very near approximation to the truth.

The profits of the Bank are derived from sources which are well known. They arise, as has been already stated, from the interest on public and private deposits,—the interest on the amount of their notes in circulation, after deducting the amount of cash and bullion,—the interest on their capital and savings,—the allowance paid them for the management of the public debt,—the profits from their dealings in bullion, and from the destruction of their notes.—All these form the gross profits of the Bank, from which must be deducted only their expences, the stamp duty, and the property tax, in order to ascertain their net profits.

Under the head of expences must be included all the charges attending the management of the national debt, as well as those incurred by the proper business of the Bank.—In estimating the former of these charges, I have already stated my grounds for believing that it could not exceed 150,000*l*.—In the management of the public business, it was stated by the committee on public expenditure, that four hundred and fifty clerks were employed in 1807; and it is probable that the number may now be increased to between five and six hundred.

It has also I understand been stated from the best authority, in parliament, that the Bank employed in the whole of their establishment about one thousand clerks; consequently if five hundred are employed exclusively on the public business, five hundred more must be engaged in the business of the Bank.—Supposing now the expences to bear some regular proportion to the number of clerks employed; as 150,000*l.* has been calculated to be the expence attending the employment of five hundred clerks in the public business, we may estimate a like expence to be incurred by the employment of the other five hundred, and therefore, the whole expences of the Bank to be at the present time about 300,000*l.*, including all charges whatsoever *.

But although this large sum is now expended, it must have been of gradual growth since 1797; when, probably, the whole expences of the establishment were not more than one-half the present amount. In the first place, since 1797, the amount of Bank notes in circulation has in-

* It has been remarked that a sufficient allowance is not made in my calculations for the losses of the Bank by bad debts, in consequence of the bad bills which they occasionally discount. Their losses from this source, I am told, are often very large. On the other hand, I have been informed that the profits of the Bank, from private deposits, for which I have taken no credit, must be considerable, as the East India Company, and many other public boards, keep their cash at the Bank.

A deduction from the Bank profits should have been made for their loss by Aslett, and for the expences attending their military corps. My argument will not be affected by their surplus capital being only 12 or 11 instead of 13 millions. *Note to Second Edition.*

creased from about twelve millions to twenty-
eight millions, but the expences of their circulation, instead of increasing in the same proportion only, have, at least, increased as one to ten.

The amount of notes of five pounds and upwards has been raised from twelve to eighteen
millions, and if the average value of notes, of all
descriptions above five pounds, be even so low as
fifteen pounds, a circulation of twelve millions
would consist of 800,000 notes, and a circulation
of 18 millions of 1,200,000 notes, an increase in
the proportion, as one to one and one-half,
but the nine millions of notes under five pounds,
which are now in circulation, have been wholly
created since 1797, and if they consist of five
millions of notes of one pound, and two millions
of notes of two pounds, a number of seven millions of notes has been further added to the
circulation, and the whole number of notes
has been raised since 1797, from 800,000 to
8,200,000, or as one to ten, and at an expence
ten times greater than was incurred at that
time, the expence being in proportion to the
number, and not to the amount of notes. It
is probable too, that the notes of one and two
pounds, which are so constantly used in the circulation, are more often renewed than notes of
a higher value.

The public debt, too, under the management

of the Bank, is more than doubled since 1797, and must have added considerably to the expences of that department. These expences have been already calculated to have risen since 1796, from 84,500*l.* to 150,000*l.* or 65,500*l.**

The public deposits too are at least double what they were in 1797, from all which I have a right to infer, that the expences of the Bank in 1797, could not have exceeded 150,000*l.*, and that they have been gradually increasing since that period; perhaps at the rate of seven or eight thousand pounds per ann.

The next subject for consideration, is the amount of cash and bullion in the Bank, which at no time has been laid before the public;— that, and the amount of their discounts, were the only material facts which the Bank concealed from the public in the eventful year 1797. —They stated in the account laid before parliament, that their cash and bullion, and their bills and notes discounted, amounted together to 4,176,080*l.* on the 26th of *February* 1797. They gave also a scale of discounts from 1782 to 1797, and a scale of the cash and bullion in the

* The Committee on public expenditure calculated these expences at 119,500*l.* in 1807, and stated the increase from 1796 to 1807 at about 35,000*l.*

Bank for the same period. By comparing these tables with each other, and with some parts of the evidence delivered before the parliamentary committees, an ingenious calculator discovered the whole secret which the Bank wished to conceal According to his table the cash and bullion in the Bank, on the 26th of *February* 1797, was reduced as low as 1,227,000*l.*,—and four millions was about the sum which the Bank considered as fair cash; to which it never attained after *December* 1795, though previously to that year it was on some occasions more than double that amount.

For the first year or two after the suspension of cash payments, the Bank must have made great efforts to replenish their coffers with cash and bullion, as they were then by no means sure that they should not be again required to pay their notes in specie. We find accordingly, by accounts returned to parliament by the mint, that the amount of gold coined in 1797 and 1798, was very little less in value than 5,000,000*l.**

* The committee of secrecy reported to parliament, that the cash and bullion in the Bank, in *November* 1797, had increased to an amount more than five times the value of that at which they stood on the 25th of *February* 1797. They stated too, that the bankers and traders of London,

Whatever might have been the amount of cash and bullion, which the Bank had acquired in the first two years after the suspension of cash payments, it is probable that their stock has been decreasing since that period, as they could have no motive for keeping a large amount of such unproductive capital, when they must have been quite secure that no call could be made on them by the holders of their notes for guineas, and that before they were again required to pay in specie, they would have ample notice to prepare a due store of the precious metals.—It does not appear possible then, under all the circumstances of the case, that the Bank can have added to their stock of bullion, since the great coinages of 1797 and 1798; but it is highly probable that they have considerably reduced it.

In estimating the profits of the Bank, as far as those profits are influenced by their stock of cash and bullion, I shall be justified in considering them greater since 1797 and 1798, as since those years they would naturally keep a

who had a right, by the act of parliament, to demand three-fourths of any deposit in cash, which they had made in the Bank, of five hundred pounds and upwards, after the 25th of *February* 1797, had only claimed in *November* 1797, about one-sixteenth.

less part of their capital in that unproductive shape, and, consequently, more in Exchequer bills, or in merchants' acceptances, securities which pay interest, and are productive of profit. —On an average of the whole eighteen years, from 1797 to 18:5, the cash and bullion of the Bank cannot be estimated as amounting to more than three millions, though, probably, for the first year or two, it amounted to four or five millions.

These circumstances being premised, it will not be difficult to calculate the profits of the Bank, from 1797 to the present time, all the facts necessary to such calculation being known to us excepting the two I have just stated, viz. the amount of expences and of cash and bullion, but which cannot differ much from that at which I have calculated them.

Proceeding then on this basis, it appears, as will be seen by the accounts in the Appendix, that the profits and surplus capital of the Bank for a series of years, after paying all dividends and bonuses, have been as follows :

Year commencing in January	Surplus capital.	Profits after paying dividend and bonuses.	Dividend and bonus together.
1797	£3,826,890	£ 89,872	7 per cent.
1798	3,916,762	533,621	7 do.
1799	4,450,383	*	17 do.
1800	3,941,228	611,981	7 do.
1801	4,553,209	116,038	12 do.
1802	4,669.247	160,509	9½ do.
1803	5,129,756	765,859	7 do.
1804	5,895,615	306,794	12 do.
1805	6,202,409	346,335	12 do.
1806	6,548,744	368,008	12 do.
1807	6.916,752	581,274	10 do.
1808	7,498,026	385,855	10 do.
1809	7,883.891	470,760	10 do.
1810	8,354,651	651,483	10 do.
1811	9,006,134	722,188	10 do.
1812	9,728,322	739,867	10 do.
1813	10,468,189	809,786	10 do.
1814	11,279,975	1,081,649	10 do.
1815	12,359,624	1,066,625	
1816	13,426,249		

If in the accounts referred to, it should be thought that I have estimated the expences of the Bank too low, it may on the other hand be remarked that I have not allowed for any profit from the deposits of individuals. Those deposits may not be very large, as the Bank do not afford the same accommodation to individuals as given by other bankers. Some profit must, however, be made from this source, as well as from the loss and destruction of notes, which it may be presumed, after a time, are not in-

* There was this year a loss of 509,155l.

cluded in the amount stated to be in circulation. By the purchase of silver, and coinage of tokens, the Bank must, on the whole, have been gainers; for the value of the token has been generally lower in the market, than it has passed for in circulation at the time of its issue.

In point of fact, too, the Bank receives more than five per cent. interest for their money; for Exchequer bills, paying three pence half-penny per day, pay 5*l.* 6*s.* 5½*d.* per cent. per ann.; and, in discounting bills, the interest being immediately deducted, is employed as capital, and is instantly productive of profit; at the same time, it must be observed that during a part of the time for which these calculations are made, Exchequer bills bore an interest of only three pence farthing per day, which amounts to 4*l.* 18*s.* 0¼*d.* per cent. per ann., rather less than five per cent.

In *March* 1801, when a bonus of five per cent., in navy five per cents., was divided amongst the proprietors of Bank stock, Mr. Tierney said in the house of commons, " that when " the affairs of the Bank of England were " investigated by the house of commons in " 1797, the surplus profits were considered " by some as a security for the engagements of " the Bank to the public." To which Mr. Samuel Thornton. then governor of the Bank, replied, that " he could assure the honourable " member, that the security of the public would " not be lessened from what it was·in 1797, by " the division of the sum of 582,120*l.* voted at " the general court, on the 19th instant, as ex-" clusive of that sum, the surplus profits of the " Bank were more now than they were in " 1797*."

On an inspection of the account in the Appendix, it will be seen, that after paying all the dividends and bonuses to the proprietors, the Bank had accumulated in *April* 1801, savings to the amount of 3,945,109*l.* exceeding the savings of 1797, by 118,219*l.*, an increase not inconsistent with the declaration of Mr. Thornton, and therefore tending to confirm the correctness of the basis on which these calculations are made. †

It will appear on an examination of the accounts in the Appendix for the subsequent years, that the profits of the Bank for every year,

* Allardyce's Address to the proprietors of the Bank of England, Appendix, No. 11.

† The accounts in the Appendix are made up from *Jan.* to *Jan.* The bonus in question was paid in *April* 1801. The net profits of the Bank for the whole year 1801 were

since 1801, have exceeded the annual dividend paid to the proprietors, and that in 1815, the surplus for that year only must have amounted to 1,066,625*l.* so that the Bank could have paid a dividend for that year of nineteen per cent., instead of ten per cent.

It will appear too that if the Bank affairs have been only moderately well managed, they must now have an accumulated fund of no less than thirteen millions, which, in defiance of the clearest language of an act of parliament, the di-

1,526,019*l.*, consequently for the quarter, ending in *April*, they may be stated at - - - -		£ 381,504
Which, added to the surplus capital of *January* 1801 - - -		4,553,209
Gives the total of the surplus capital in *April* 1801, before paying the dividend and bonus - -		4,934,713
Deduct		
Dividend three and a half per cent., for half a year - - -	407,484	
Bonus five per cent. - - -	582,120	
		989,604
Leaving a surplus capital in *April*, 1801, of - - -		3,945,109
And exceeding that in 1797 of -		3,826,890
by		£ 118,219

rectors have hitherto withheld from the proprietors.

With such an accumulated fund, the Bank could make a division of one hundred per cent. bonus, without infringing on their permanent capital: and if they could maintain their present profits, with a deduction only of 523,908*l.* per ann. the interest (less income tax) on the surplus capital proposed to be divided, they would still have an unappropriated income of 542,000*l.* which would enable them to increase their permanent dividend from ten to fourteen and a half per cent., in addition to the bonus of one hundred per cent.

If they divided only a bonus of seventy-five per cent. they would retain a surplus capital, exceeding that of 1797, and might on the above supposition have an unappropriated income of 673,000*l.* —they might therefore raise their permanent dividend from ten to fifteen and a half per cent., in addition to the bonus of seventy-five per cent.

But it cannot be expected that the Bank will, during peace, have the same opportunities of making profit as during war, and the proprietors must prepare themselves for a considerable reduction in their annual income. What that reduction may be will depend on the new agreement now to be entered into with government; on the future amount of public deposits; and

on the conditions on which the restoration of
metallic payments may be enforced. It is evident that if the plan which I have recommended
in the fourth section of this work be adopted,
the Bank profits from this last item will not be
materially reduced.

Supposing, however, that the reduction of the
annual income of the Bank should, from the
falling off of their profits in all these departments, be as much as 500,000*l.*, the profits of
the Bank would, nevertheless, be equal to the
payment of the present permanent dividend of
ten per cent., even after a division of one hundred per cent. bonus to the proprietors of Bank
stock; for, if my calculations be correct, the
profits of the Bank, after the payment of the
annual dividend of ten per cent. to the proprietors, were for the year ending *January* 1st,
1816 - - - - - £1,066,625

Deduct then the interest now made on 11,642,400*l.* proposed to be divided, less property tax - - - -	523,908	
Loss by a peace arrangement	500,000	1,023,908
Leaving a surplus of, per ann.		£42,717

If, instead of a hundred per cent., fifty per
cent. bonus only were paid to the proprietors,

the annual surplus profit of the Bank, after paying ten per cent. dividend, would be 304,671*l.* a sum equal to a permanent increase of dividend of two and a half per cent.

And if no bonus whatever were paid, but the savings were considered as part of the Bank capital, the annual surplus profit of the Bank, after paying ten per cent. dividend, would be 566,625*l.*, very nearly equal to a permanent increase of dividend of five per cent.

These estimates are made on a supposition too, that the property tax should permanently continue, which is calculated to be an annual charge of more than 200,000*l*, to the Bank, and consequently more than equal to a dividend of one and three quarters per cent.

But the Directors are bound, in my opinion, under every case, to divide the surplus profits amongst the proprietors, the law imperatively enjoining such a division, and policy being no wise opposed to it.

Well was it urged by the Hon. Mr. Bouverie, who moved in the last Bank court that an account of the surplus capital of the Bank be laid before the proprietors, that this law respecting the division of profits was probably enacted by the legislature, on a consideration of the powers of accumulation at compound interest, and the dangers which might arise to the constitution or the country, from any corporation becoming possessed of millions of treasure. If the profits of the Bank were to continue at the present rate, and no addition were to be made to the dividend now paid of ten per cent., the accumulation of the surplus profits in forty years would give to the Bank a disposable fund of more than one hundred and twenty millions. Wisely then did the legislature enact, that " All the profits, benefits, " and advantage from time to time arising out " of the management of the said corporation, " shall (the charges of managing the business " of the said governor and company *only ex-* " *cepted)* be applied from time to time to the " uses of all the members of the said corporation " for the time being, rateably and in proportion " to each member's part, share, and interest, in " the common capital, and principal stock, of " the said governor and company of the Bank of " England."

Those who vindicated the directors at the last general court for their departure from the line of conduct prescribed by the law, recommended the increase of the capital of the Bank,—and they thought that the accumulated savings might be advantageously employed for such purpose.

It is said that the Bank directors are favourable to such a plan.

If the measure should be a good one, the sum of capital to be added should be at once defined,—the proprietors should have accounts laid before them of the amount of their accumulated fund, and should be consulted on the expediency of such a disposition of it,—and lastly the sanction of Parliament should be obtained.

The Bank, however, have waited for none of these conditions,—they have been, in fact, for years adding the annual surplus profits to their capital, without defining the amount added, or to be added; they do it without laying any accounts before the proprietors—without consulting them; and not only without the sanction of Parliament, but in defiance of an express law on the subject.

But if the Bank complied with all these conditions, would the measure itself be expedient, and are the reasons given in support of it, namely the enlarged business of the Bank, and that it would tend to the security both of the Bank and the public, of sufficient weight to justify its adoption ?

The business and income of the Bank depend, as before stated, on the amount of the aggregate fund which they have to employ, and this

fund is derived from the three following sources:
The amount of Bank notes in circulation, deducting only the cash and bullion: The amount of public and private deposits: And the amount of that part of the capital of the Bank which is not lent to government. But it is only the two former of these funds which contribute to the real profit of the Bank; for the interest, received for surplus capital, being only five per cent., might be made with as much facility by each individual proprietor, on his share of such capital, if under his own management, as by combining the whole into one fund. If the proprietors were to add from their own individual property ten millions to the capital of the Bank, the income of the Bank would indeed be increased 500,000*l.* or five per cent. on ten millions; but the proprietors would not be gainers by such an arrangement. If, however, ten millions were added to the amount of notes, and could be permanently maintained in circulation, —or if the public and private deposits were to be increased ten millions, the *income* of the Bank would not only be increased 500,000*l.*, but their *real profits* also, and this advantage would arise wholly from their acting as a joint company, and could not be otherwise obtained.

There is this material difference between a Bank and all other trades: A Bank would

never be established, if it obtained no other
profits but those from the employment of its
own capital : its real advantage commences
only when it employs the capital of others.
Other trades, on the contrary, often make enormous profits by the employment of their own
capital only.

But if this argument be correct, with respect
to an additional capital to be actually raised
from amongst the proprietors, it is equally so to
one withheld from them.

To increase the *profits* of the Bank proprietors, then, an increase of capital would be
neither necessary nor desirable.

Neither would such an addition contribute
towards the *security* of the Bank; for the Bank
can never be called upon for more than the
payment of their notes, and the public and private deposits; these constituting at all times,
the whole of their debts. After paying away
their cash and bullion, their remaining securities, consisting of merchants acceptances and
Exchequer bills, must be at least equal to the
value of their debts; and in no case can these
securities be deficient, even without *any* surplus
capital, excepting the Bank should lose all that
which constitutes their growing dividend; and
even then they could not be distressed, unless

we suppose that at the same time payment were demanded for every note in circulation, and for the whole of their deposits, both public and private.

Is it against such a contingency that the proprietors are called upon to provide; when even under these, almost impossible circumstances, the Bank would have an untouched fund of 11,686,000*l*., which Government owe them?

Would the security of the public be increased? In one respect it would. If the Bank have no other capital but that which they lend to Government, they must lose all that capital by their trade, or more than eleven millions and a half, before the public can be sufferers; but if the capital of the Bank were doubled, the Bank might lose twenty-three millions, before any creditor of theirs could suffer loss. Are the friends to an increase of the capital of the Bank prepared to say, that it is against the consequences of the loss of the whole Bank capital that they are desirous of protecting the public?

It remains to be considered, whether the ability of the Bank to pay their notes in specie would be increased by an increase of their capital. The ability of the Bank, to pay their notes in specie, must depend upon the proportion of specie which they may keep, to meet the probable demand for payment of their notes; and in this respect their power cannot be increased, for they may now, *if they please*, have a stock of specie, not only equal to all their notes in circulation, but to the whole of the public and private deposits, and under no possible circumstances can more be demanded of them. But the profits of the Bank essentially depend on the smallness of the stock of cash and bullion; and the whole dexterity'of the business consists in maintaining the largest possible circulation, with the least possible amount of their funds in the unprofitable shape of cash and bullion. The amount of notes in circulation depends in no degree on the amount of capital possessed by the issuers of notes, but on the amount required for the circulation of the country; which is regulated, as I have before attempted to shew, by the value of the standard, the amount of payments, and the economy practised in effecting them.

The only effect then of the increase of the capital of the Bank would be to enable them to lend to government or to merchants those funds, which would otherwise have been lent by individuals of the community. The Bank would have more business to do—they would accumulate more merchants acceptances and Exchequer bills: they would even increase the income of the Bank; but the profits of the proprietors would be neither more nor less, if the market rate of interest for money were at five per cent., and the business of the Bank were carried on with the same economy. The proprietors would be positive losers, if they could individually have employed their shares of this capital. in trade, or otherwise, at a greater profit.

But not only do the Bank refuse, in direct contradiction to an act of parliament, to make a division of their accumulated profits, but they are equally determined not to communicate to the proprietors what those profits are, notwithstanding their bye-law enjoins, " that twice in " every year a general court shall be called, and " held for considering *the general state and con-* " *dition of this corporation*, and for the making of " dividends, *out of all and singular* the produce " and profit of the capital stock and fund of this. ". corporation and the trade thereof, amongst " the several owners and proprietors therein, " according to their several shares and propor- " tions."

If the law had been silent on the subject, the Bank Directors would, I think, be bound to shew some specific evil which would result from publicity, before they refused to shew a statement of their affairs to the proprietors.

It is in fact the only security which the proprietors have, against the abuse of the trust reposed in the Directors.

The affairs of the Bank may not always be managed by such men as are now in the Direction, against whom not a shadow of suspicion any where exists.

Without accounts; without a division of profits; and without any other proof of the accumulated fund of the Bank, but the notoriety of the increase of the sources from which the Bank profits are made—and that for a period of more than ten years; what security have the proprietors, against a corrupt administration of their affairs? It is not consistent with the delicacy of the situation of those who are entrusted with the management of millions to demand such unbounded confidence—so much reliance on their own personal character, without stating some grounds for such a demand. Yet the only answer which the Directors made to a motion for a statement of profits, in the last general court, was, that they should consider the passing of such a resolution as betraying a want of confidence in them, and as a censure on their proceedings.

On all sides, such an intention was disclaimed; yet, strange to say, no other reply could be obtained from the Directors.

The publication of accounts, besides being necessary as a check against the *corrupt* administration of the Directors, is also necessary to give assurance to the proprietors, that their affairs are *ably* administered. Since 1797, no statement has been made of the condition of the Bank; and, even in that year, it was made to Parliament, on a particular exigence, and not to the proprietors of Bank stock. How then, can the proprietors know whether, in the favourable circumstances in which the Bank have been placed, the directors have availed themselves of all the opportunities which have offered, of employing the funds entrusted to their charge to the best advantage? Would it not be desirable, that from time to time the proprietors should be able to ascertain whether their just expectations had been realised, and whether their affairs had been ably as well as honourably administered? If the practice of laying all accounts before the proprietors had been always followed, perhaps the Directors of 1793, 1794, and 1795, might have been admonished for so badly managing the affairs of the Bank, as to keep permanently in their coffers a sum of cash and bullion, generally more than three-fourths, and seldom less than one-half the whole amount of their notes in circulation. They might possibly have been told, that such a waste of the resources of the Bank shewed a very limited knowledge of the principles by which a paper currency should be regulated.*

These irregularities in the proceedings of the Bank excited the attention of an independent proprietor, Mr. Allardyce, in 1797 and 1801. In his excellent publication on Bank affairs, he has pointed out with great force and ability the illegal conduct of the Bank. His opinion was confirmed by Mr., now Sir James, Mansfield, who was consulted by him as to the course, necessary to be pursued, to compel the directors to lay an account before the proprietors of the state of the company. Sir James Mansfield's opinion was given as follows:

" I am of opinion, that *every* proprietor, at a
" general half yearly court, has a *right* to re-
" quire from the directors, and it is the *duty* of
" the latter to produce, all such accounts, books

---

* For the account of cash and bullion in the Bank in the above years I trust to the calculations to which I have already alluded, page 74. I can see no reason to doubt their general accuracy.

" and papers, as are necessary to enable the
" proprietors to judge of the state and condition
" of the corporation and its funds, and to deter-
" mine what dividend ought to be paid. The
" proper method to be pursued by those who
" consult me in order to obtain such a produc-
" tion is, that a number of respectable proprie-
" tors should immediately give notice to the
" governor and other directors, that they shall
" require at the next general court a production
" of all the necessary books, accounts and pa-
" pers; and at the general court, when it shall
" be held, to attend and require such a produc-
" tion. If it shall not be obtained, I then advise
" them immediately, or within a few days after
" the holding of the general court, to make an
" application to the governor to call a general
" court, which application must be made by
" nine members at least, having each 500*l.*
" stock. If the governor shall refuse to call such
" general court, then the nine members who
" shall have applied to him to have a court call-
" ed, may themselves call one in the manner
" prescribed by the charter ; and whether the
" governor calls such court, or it is called by the
" nine members, I advise them, as soon as it is
" called, to apply to the court of King's Bench

" for a mandamus to the governor and directors,
" to produce at such court all the necessary
" books, accounts and papers.

"J. MANSFEILD."
'" Temple, March 9, 1801."

In consequence of this opinion, Mr. Allardyce
delivered a demand in writing at the next general court, held the 19th March, 1801, that the
accounts should be produced, and no doubt in-
tended to follow up this proceeding in the way
recommended by Sir James Mansfield,—but he
soon after died; and since that time no proprietor has made any demand for accounts, till at
the last general court in December. It is re-
markable that, very unexpectedly to the proprietors, a bonus of 5 per cent., in navy 5 per Cents.,
was voted in the general court of the 19th March,
1801, the day on which Mr. Allardyce's demand
was made and refused. The first motion for accounts made by Mr. Allardyce was in the general court, held 14th Dec. 1797; and in March
1799, there was a bonus of 10 per cent. in 5
per Cents. 1797. Mr. Allardyce did not, I believe, make any motion in the Bank court between December, 1797, and March, 1801.

Since 1797, then, the proprietors have remain-
ed in utter ignorance of the affairs of the Bank.
During eighteen years the directors have been

H

silently enjoying their lucrative trade, and may
now possibly think that the same course is best
adapted to the interests of the Bank, particularly
as negociations are about to take place with
government, when it might be as well that the
amount of their accumulated fund should not
be known. But the public attention has been
lately called to the affairs of the Bank; and the
subject of their profits is generally canvassed
and understood. Publicity would now probably
be more beneficial than hurtful to the Bank; for
exaggerated accounts of their profits have been
published which may raise extravagant expectations, and which may be best corrected by
official statements. Besides which, the Bank
are secure of their charter for seventeen years to
come; and the public cannot, during that time,
deprive them of the most profitable part of their
trade. If indeed the charter were about to
expire, the public might question the policy of
permitting a company of merchants to enjoy all
the advantages which attend the supplying of a
great country with paper money; and although
they would naturally look with jealousy, after
the experience furnished by other states, to
allowing that power to be in the hands of government, they might probably think that in a
free country means might be found by which

so considerable an advantage might be obtained for the state, independently of all control of ministers. Paper money may be considered as affording a seignorage equal to its whole exchangeable value, — but seignorage in all countries belongs to the state, and with the security of convertibility as proposed in the former part of this work, and the appointment of commissioners responsible to parliament only, the state, by becoming the sole issuer of paper money, in town as well as in the country, might secure a net revenue to the public of no less than two millions sterling. Against this danger, however, the Bank is secure till 1833, and therefore on every ground publicity is expedient.

APPENDIX.

No. I.*

Table shewing the Amount annually paid by the Public, from 1797 to 1815, for Management of the British, Irish, German, and Portuguese Debt.

Year commencing 5th January.		L.	s.	d.
1797	. . . .	162,431	5	3
1798	. . . .	212,592	1	5
1799	. . . .	218,190	17	0
1800	. . . .	238,294	3	8
1801	. . . .	236,772	15	8
1802	. . . .	263,105	14	6
1803	. . . .	247,538	11	0
1804	. . . .	267,786	19	7
1805	. . . .	271,911	11	9
1806	. . . .	292,127	9	10
1807	. . . .	297,757	16	1
1808	. . . .	210,549	2	7
1809	. . . .	222,775	2	4
1810	. . . .	217,825	13	5
1811	. . . .	228,349	16	0
1812	. . . .	223,705	12	5
1813	. . . .	238,827	17	7
1814	. . . .	242,263	14	7

* The particulars in the above table are taken from the annual finance book, printed by order of the house of commons. They include not only what is paid to the Bank, but to the Exchequer and South Sea company. The annual charge of the South Sea company is now about 14,560*l.* In 1797 it was 14,657*l.* The Exchequer charge was as high as 6760*l.* 6*s.* 8*d.*, in 1807 it fell gradually to 2485*l.* and has now, I believe, ceased.

The Bank have also been paid for management of life annuities since 1810,—and since 1812, about 1200*l.* or 1300*l.* per ann. for management of a loan of two and half millions, raised for the East India Company, which are not included in this table.

No. II.

Table shewing the Amount annually received by the Bank from 1797 to 1815, for receiving Contributions on Loans.*

Year commencing Michaelmas.	L.	s.	d.
1796	20,506	3	4
1797	27,410	0	4
Year commencing 5th January.			
1799	16,115	6	8
1800	12,489	15	5
1801	39,080	17	11
1802	22,538	12	3
1803	9669	10	0
1804			
1805	11,683	19	7
1806	18,130	16	3
1807	16,115	16	8
1808	12,650	18	7
1809	8,400	0	0
1810	11,080	0	0
1811	14,705	0	0
1812 . . .	19,031	14	0
1813	21,639	8	9
1814	42,200	0	C

* This table is taken from an account laid before parliament, on the 19th of June 1815.

No. III.

The total Amount of the Unredeemed Funded Debt of Great
Britain and Ireland, including Loans to the Emperor of
Germany and Prince Regent of Portugal, payable in Great
Britain, was on the first of February 1815, according to ac-
counts laid before parliament - *L.*727,767,421 2 5
Do. for East India Company - - 3,929,561 0 0

　　　　　　　　　　　　　　　　　 731,696,982 2 5¼

Debt contracted from⎫
　Feb. 1 to Aug. 1, ⎬87,448,402 16
　1815 - - - ⎭
Redeemed from Feb. ⎱11,099,166 0
　1 to Aug. 1, 1815 ⎰

　　　　　　　　　　　　　 76,349,236 16 0

Total of unredeemed funded debt on
　Aug. 1, 1815 - - - - - L.808,046,218 18 5¼

The charge for Management on which is as follows:

*L.*15,233,484 13 11　South Sea stock and annuities, for the
　　　　　　　　　　　management of which the South
　　　　　　　　　　　Sea Co. is paid *L.* 14,560 4 11
11,686,000 0 0　due to the Bank of⎱
　　　　　　　　　　England - -⎰ 5,898 3 5
600,000,000 0 0　at 340*l.* per million　204,000 0 0
181,126.734 4 6¼　at 300*l.* do.　54,338 0 5

808,046.218 18　5¼
2,795,340 0 0　life annuities - -　899 5 0
39,735,898 6 8　for 1,589,435*l.* 6*s.* 8*d.* ⎫
　　　　　　　　　　anns. at 25 years ⎬11,920 15 4
───────────　purchase　-　 ⎭
L.850,577,457 5 1¼

　　　　　　　　　　　　　　　291,616 9 7
Deduct the first sum paid to the South ⎱
　Sea Company - - - - -⎰ 14,560 4 11

Management paid to the Bank of England ⎱
　on the Debt as it stood Aug. 1, 1815. ⎰ 277,056 4 8

No. IV.

Average Amount of Bank of England Notes, including Bank Post Bills, in circulation in each of the following years.

	Notes of five pounds, and upwards, including Bank post bills.	Notes under five pounds.	Total.
1797	10,095,620	1,096,100	11,191,720
1798	11,527,250	1,807,502	13,334,752
1799	12,408,522	1,653,805	14,062,327
1800	13,598,666	2,243,266	15,841,932
1801	13,454,367	2,715,182	16,169,594
1802	13,917,977	3,136,477	17,054,454
1803	12,983,477	3,864,045	16,847,522
1804	12,621,348	4,723,672	17,345,020
1805	12,697,352	4,544,580	17,241,932
1806	12,844,170	4,291,230	17,135,400
1807	13,221,988	4,183,013	17,405,001
1808	13,402,160	4,132,420	17,534,580
1809	14,133,615	4,868,275	19,001,890
1810	16,085,522	6,644,763	22,730,285*
1811	16,286,950	7,260,575	23,547,525
1812	15,862,120	7,600,000	23,462,120
1813	16,057,000	8,030,000	24,087,000
1814	18,540,780	9,300,000	27,840,780
1815	18,157,956	9,161,454	27,319,410

* Till 1811, the above are extracted from the report of the bullion committee; since that year from returns made to parliament.

No. V.

An Estimate of the Profits of the Bank of England, for the year commencing Jan. 5, 1797.

Bank notes in circulation L.11,191,720
Public deposits -   -   -   5,000,000
Surplus above permanent }
 capital * -   -   -   -}   3,826,890
       —————
       20,018,610
Deduct cash and bullion   5,000,000
       —————

Funds yielding interest - 15,018,610 at 5 p. c.   750,930
Charge for management of national debt - - -   143,800
 Do. - do. - Loan - - -   20,506
 Do. - do. - Lottery - -   1,000
Interest on 11,686,000l. lent to government at }
 three per cent - - - - - -}   350,604
           —————
           L.1,266,840
     Deduct
Expences -   -   -   - L.150,000
Stamps .   -   -   -   -   12,000
Voluntary contribution   -   - 200,000
        —————
          362,000
          —————
          904,840
Dividend seven per cent. on L.11,642,400 -   814,968
          —————
      Profit - L.89,872

Estimate for the year commencing January 1798.

Surplus before 1797 - - L.3,826,890
Do. - of 1797 - -   89,872
       —————
       3,916,762
Bank notes in circulation   13,334,752
Public deposits   -   -   5,700,000
       —————
       22,951,514
Deduct cash and bullion - 4,000,000
       —————
Funds yielding interest - 18,951,514 at 5 p. c. 947,575

———————————————————

* This sum was returned by the Bank to parliament as their surplus capital, February 26, 1797.

Brought over - - - - L.947,575
Charge for management of national debt 192,000
Do. Loans - - - - 27,410
Do. Lottery - - - 1,000
                                              ————— 220,410
Interest on 11,686,800*l.* capital at 3 p. c. - - 350,604
                                              1,518,589

 Deduct
Expences - - - - 158,000
Stamps - - - - 12,000
Seven per cent. dividend - 814,968
                                              ————— 984,968
       Profit - 533,621

YEAR COMMENCING JANUARY 5, 1799.

Former savings - - L.3,916,762
Do. for 1798 - - 533,621
                        ————————
                        4,450,383
Bank notes - - 14,062,300
Public deposits - - 6,400,000
                        ————————
                        24,912,683
Deduct cash and bullion 3,000,000
Funds yielding interest - 21,912,683   ·5 p. c. 1,095,634
Charge for management of ⎫ - 196,700
 national debt - ⎭
Do. Loans - - - - 16,115
Do. Lotteries - - - 1000
                                      ————— 213,815
Interest on 11,686,800*l.* - - - - 350,604
                                      1,660,053

 Deduct
Expences - - - - 166,000
Stamps* - - - - 24,000
Dividend seven per cent - 814,968
Bonus ten per cent - - 1,164,240
                                      ————— 2,169,208
      Loss - 509,155

* The composition for stamps was raised this year to 24,000*l.*—in
1803-4, to 32,000*l.*—in 1806-7, to 42,000*l.*—and in 1815-16, to 87,500*l.*

YEAR COMMENCING JANUARY 5, 1800.

Former savings	- -	L.4,450,383
Loss of 1799	- -	509,155
		3,941,228
Bank notes	- -	15,841,900
Deposits	- -	7,100,000
		26,883,128

Deduct cash and bullion }	3,000,000	
Loan to government }	3,000,000*	6,000,000

Funds yielding interest L.20,883,128 at 5 p. c.		1,044,156
Management of national debt	216,700	
Do. Loans - - -	12,489	
Do. Lottery - - -	1,000	
		230,189
Interest on 11,686,800l.		350,604
		1,624,949

Deduct		
Expences - - -	174,000	
Stamps - - -	24,000	
Dividend seven per cent. -	814,968	
		1,013,968
Profit -		£611,981

YEAR COMMENCING JANUARY 5, 1801.

Former savings -	L.3,941,228	
Surplus, 1800 -	611,981	
	4,553,209	
Bank notes -	16,169,500	
Deposits - -	7,800,000	
	28,522,709	

Loan to government }	3,000,000	
Cash and bullion }	3,000,000	6,000,000
Funds yielding interest	22,522,709 at five p. c.	1,126,135

* The Bank lent to government, this year, three millions, without interest, for six years, and afterwards continued the same loan for eight years at three per cent. interest.

```
Brought over        -        -        -      L.1,126,135
Charge for management of national debt  215,200
Do. do.  Loans    -      -      -      39,080
Do. do.  Lottery  -      -      -       1,000
                                      ─────────
                                                255,280
Interest on capital    *      *      -          350,604
                                              ─────────
        Deduct                                1,732,019
Expences    -      -      *      182,000
Stamps    -      *      *      -      -   24,000
                                      ─────────
                                                206,000
                                              ─────────
                                              1,526,019
Dividend seven per cent.    -      814,968
Bonus five per cent.    *      -   582,120
                                      ─────────
                                              1,397,088
                                              ─────────
                                                128,931
                    Property-tax*      -         12,893
                                               ─────────
                    Profit    *    -    -       116,038
                                               ─────────
```

YEAR COMMENCING JANUARY, 1802.

```
Former savings    -    -    L.4,553,209
Profits, 1801    -    :  -      116,038
                             ──────────
                              4,669,247
Bank notes    -              17,050,000
Deposits    -    -            8,600,000
                             ──────────
                             30,319,247
        Deduct
Loan to Go- }  3,000,000
    vernment }
Cash and    }  3,000,000
    bullion }
             ─────────
              6,000,000
                             ──────────
Funds yielding interest  24,319,247 at 5 p. c.  1,215,962
```

* The property-tax was paid by the proprietors till 1806, when the Bank agreed to pay, on their whole profits to Government, and not to make any deduction from the dividend warrant.

Brought over - - - - . L.		1,215,062
Charge for management of national debt	241,600	
Do. do. Loans - - - -	22,538	
Do. do. Lottery - - -	1,000	
		265,138
Interest on capital - - - - -		350,604
Deduct .		1,831,704
Expences - - - - -	190,000	
Stamps - - - - -	24,000	
Dividend seven per cent. -	814,968	
Bonus two and half per cent.	291,060	
		1,320,028
		511,676
Property tax - -		51,167
Profit - - -		460,509

YEAR COMMENCING JANUARY, 1803.

Former savings - L.	4,669.247		
Profits, 1802 - -	460 509		
	5,129,756		
Bank notes - -	16,847,500		
Deposits - -	9,300,000		
	31,277,256		
Loan to Go- } vernment }	3,000,000		
Cash and bul- } lion - - }	3,000,000		
		6,000,000	
	25,277,256		1,263,862
Management of the national debt -		226,000	
Do. do. Loans - - -		9,669	
Do. do. Lottery - - -		1,000	
			236,669
Interest on capital - - - - -			350,604
			1,851,135

Brought over - - - - - - - - L. 1,851,135
   Deduct
Expenses - - - - 198,000
Stamps - - - - 32,000
Dividend seven per cent - - 814,968

            1,044,968

            806,167
Property tax on net profit, five per cent. - 40,308

       Profit - - 705,859

YEAR COMMENCING JANUARY, 1804.

Former savings - - L. 5,129,756
Profits, 1803 - - 765,859

        5,895,615
Bank notes - - 17,345,020
Deposits - - 10,000,000

 Deduct   33,240,635·
Loan to Go- }3,000,000
 vernment
Cash and } 3,000,000
 bullion
     6,000,000

Funds yielding interest 27,240,635 five p. c. 1,362,030
Charge for management of national debt 246,700
Do. do. Loans - - - - —
Do. do. Lottery - - - 3,000
          249,700
Interest of capital - - 350,604

          1,962,334

   Deduct
Expences - - - - 206,000
Stamps - - - - 32,000
Dividend seven per cent. - - 814,968
Bonus five per cent. - - 582,120
         1,635,088

         327,246
Property tax six and a quarter per cent. - - 20,452

      Profit - - 306,794

YEAR COMMENCING 1805.

Former savings	-	L. 5,895,615
Profit, 1814	- -	306,794
		6,202,409
Bank notes	- -	17,241,932
Deposits	- - -	10,700,000
		34,144,341

Loan to Go- } 3,000,000
vernment

Cash and } 3,000,000
bullion ————— 6,000,000

	28,144,341	5 p. c.	1,407,217
Charge for management of national debt	254,400		
Do. do. Loan - - -	11,683		
Do. do. Lotteries - -	4,000		
			270,083
Interest on capital - - -			350,604
			2,027,904

Deduct

Expences - - - -	214,000	
Stamps - -	32,000	
Dividend seven per cent. - -	814,968	
Bonus five per cent. -	582,120	
		1,643,088
		384,816
Property tax ten per cent. - -		38,481
		346,335

YEAR COMMENCING 1806.

Former savings	- -	L. 6,202,409
Savings, 1805	- -	346,335
		6,548,744
Bank notes	- -	17,135,400
Public deposits	-	11,000,000
		34,684,144

Brought over   L.34,684,144

Loan to Go- } 3,000,000   at 3 p. c.*   90,000
vernment

Cash and } 3,000,000
bullion

         ———   6,000,000

         28,684,144 at 5 p. c. 1,434,207

Charge for management of national debt 275,000
Do. do.   Loan   -   -   18,130
Do. do.   Lotteries   -   -   -   2,000

                 ———   290,130

Interest on capital   -   -   -   350,604

                         2,169,941

       Deduct
Expences   -   -   222,000
Stamps   -   -   32,000
Dividend of seven per cent.   814,968
Bonus of five per cent.   -   582,120

                 ———   1,651,088

                         518,853

Property tax ten per cent. on surplus   -   51,885
†Do. ten per cent. on bonus and Oct. } 98,960
dividend   -   -   -   -

                 ———   150,845

               Profit   -   368,008

YEAR COMMENCING JANUARY, 1807.

Former savings   -   L.6,548,744
   Profit, 1806   -   368,008

                 6,916,752
Bank notes   -   -   17,405,000
Deposits   -   -   11,000,000

                 35,321,752

* See note, p. 107.   † See note, p. 106.

Brought over		35,321,752	
Loan to Government }	3,000,000	at 3 p. c.	90,000
Cash and bullion - }	3,000,000		
		6,000,000	
		29,321,752	1,466,087
			1,556,087

Management of national debt	280,500	
Do. do. Loans - -	16,115	
Do. do. Lotteries - -	5,000	
Commission for receiving property tax	3,154	
		304,769
Interest in capital - - -		350,604
		2,211,400

Deduct		
Expences - - -	230,000	
Stamps - - -	42,000	
		272,000
Dividend ten per cent. - -	1,164,240	1,939,460
Property tax - - .- - -	193 946	
		1,358,186
	Profit - -	581,274

YEAR COMMENCING 1808.

Former savings -	6,916,752	
Profit, 1807 - -	581,274	
	7,498,026	
Bank notes -	17,534,580	
Deposits - -	11,000,000	
	36,032,606	

Loan to Government }	3,000,000	at 3 per c.	90,000
Ditto	3,000,000		
Cash and bullion }	3,000,000		
	9,000,000		
	27,032,606		1,351,630
			1,441,630

I

```
Brought over    -    -    -    -    -    L. 1,441,630
Management of national debt      -    193,300
                        Loan    -     12,650
                        Lotteries  -   2,000
Commission for receiving property duty   3,154
                                         ————
                                                     211,104
Interest on capital    -    -    -    -    -          350,604
                                                   —————
                                                   2,003,338
Expences   -    -    -    -    -      239,000
Stamps     -    -    -    -    -       42,000
                                      ————
                                                     281,000
                                                   —————
                                                   1,722,338
Dividend, 10 per cent.   -   1,164,240
Property tax, ditto      -     172,233
                             ————
                                                   1,336,473
                   Profit                            385,865
                                                   ══════
```

YEAR COMMENCING JANUARY, 1809.

```
Former savings   -    -    -7,498,026
Profit, 1808     -    -  -    385,865
                             ————
                           7,883,891
Bank notes     -    -    19,000,000
Deposits       -    -    11,000,000
                         —————
                         37,883,891
Loan to·Go-  }3,000,000      at 3 per cent.    90,000
 vernment    }
Ditto without}3,000,000
 interest    }
Cash and bul-}3,000,000
 lion   -    }
             —————  9,000,000
             —————
            28,883,891                      1,444,194
Management of national debt    -    205,500
                        Loan         8,400
                        Lotteries    3,000
Commission for receiving property duty  3,154
                                      ————
                                                   220,054
Interest on capital   -    -    -    -    -         350,604
                                                  —————
                                                  2,104,852
```

Brought over - -		_L_ 2,104,852
Expences -	246,000	
Stamps -	42,000	
		288,000
		1,816,852
Dividend 10 per cent. -	1,164,240	
Property tax - -	181,852	
		1,346,092
Profit - - -		470,760

Year commencing January 1810.

Former savings - -	_L._7,883,891	
Profit - - -	470,760	
	8,354,651	
Bank notes -	22,730,000	
Deposits - -	11,000,000	
	42,084,651	

Loan to Go-vernment } 3,000,000	at 3 per cent. 90,000	
Ditto without interest - } 3,000,000		
Cash and Bul-lion - - } 3,000,000		
——— 9,000,000		

	33,084,651	1,654,232
		1,744,232
Management of national debt,	200,800	
Loan - -	11,680	
Lotteries -	3,000	
Commission for receiving property tax	3,154	
		218,634
Interest on capital - - - -		350,604
		2,313,470

Brought over - - - - - - L. 2,313,470

Deduct

Expences	- 254,000	
Stamps -	- 42,000	
		296,000
		2,017,470

Dividend, 10 per cent. - - 1,164,240
Property duty - - - 201,747

| | | 1,365,987 |

Profit - - - - 651,483

YEAR COMMENCING JANUARY 1811.

Former savings - - L. 8,354,651
1810 - - - 651,483

9,006,134
Bank notes - - 23,547,000
Deposits - - - 11,000,000

43,553,134

Loan to Go-
vernment } 3,000,000   at 3 per cent. 90,000
Ditto without }
interest - { 3,000,000
Cash and bul- }
lion - - { 3,000,000

9,000,000

34,553,134   1,727,765

1,817,765

Management of national debt, 211.300
Loan - - 14.705
Lotteries - - 4,000
Life annuities - - 206
Commission for receiv-
ing property duty 3,454

233,662
Interest on capital - - - 350,604

2,402,031

```
Brought over    -   -   -   -   -   -      L.2,402,031
              Expences  -   264,000
              Stamps  -   -   42,000
                              ──────         306,000
                                           ──────────
                                           2,096,031
Dividend, 10 per cent.   -   1,164,240
Property tax   -   -   -     209,603
                              ──────         1,373,843
                                           ──────────
              Profit   -   -   -   -        722,188
                                           ══════════
```

YEAR COMMENCING JANUARY 1812.

```
Former savings   -   L.9,006,134
1811                    722,188
                     ──────────
                      9,728,322
Bank notes   -   -   23,462,000
Deposits     -   -   11,000,000
                     ──────────
                     44,190,322
Loan to Go-  }3,000,000      at 3 per cent. 90,000
  vernment   }
Ditto without}3,000,000
  interest   }
Cash and bul-}3,000,000
  lion   -   }
             ─────── 9,000,000
                     ──────────
                     35,190,322            1,759,516
Management of national debt   -   208,000
                  Loans   -       19,031
                  Life annuities     369
Commission for receiving property duty  3,154
                              ──────         230,554
Interest on capital   -   -   -   -          350,604
                                           ──────────
                                           2,430,674
```

```
Brought over      -        -        -      L.2,430,674
            Expences    -    273,000
            Stamps      -     42,000
                             ————        315,000
                                        —————————
                                        2,115,674
Dividend, 10 per cent.   -  1,164.240
Property duty     -      -    211,567
                             ————     1,375,807
                                        —————————
            Profit     -        -         739,867
```

YEAR COMMENCING JANUARY 1813.

```
Former savings   -      -   L.9,728,322
1812       -           -        739,867
                               ——————
                              10,468,189
Bank notes      -      -     24,080,000
Deposits        -      -     11,000,000
                               ——————
                              45,548,189
Loan to Go- ⎫
 vernment  ⎬ 3,000,000        at 3 per cent.  90,000
Ditto without ⎫
 interest  -  ⎬ 3,000,000
Cash and bul- ⎫
 lion  -  -  ⎬ 3,000,000
             ———— 9,000,000
                 ————————           1,827,400
              36,548,189           ——————
                                    1,917,400

Management of national debt, 223,100
              Loan   -   -   21,639
              Ditto  -   -    2,000
              Life annuities    462
Commission for receiving property duty   3,154
                            ————       250,365
                                      ——————
                                      2,167,755
```

Brought over - - - - L.2,167 755
Interest of capital - - - - - 350,604

2,518,359

        Expences - - - 283,000
        Stamps - - - 42,000

325,000

2,193,359

Dividend, 10 per cent. - - 1,164,240
Commission for receiving property duty 219,333

1,383,573

        Profit - - - - 809,786

YEAR COMMENCING JANUARY 1814.

Former savings - - L.0,468,189
1813 - - - 809,786

11,277,975
Bank notes - - 27,840,000
Deposits - - 11,000,000

50,117,975

Loan to Go-
vernment with-} 3,000,000
out interest
Cash and bullion 3,000,000

6,000,000

44,117,975   2,205,898

Management of national debt, 227,000
Loan - - - 42,200
Life annuities - - - 576
Commission for receiving property duty 3,154

272,930
Interest of capital - - - - 350,604

2 829,432

Brought over - - - - - L.2,829,432

Expences	-	292,000
Stamps	- -	42,000
		334,000

2,495,432

Dividend, 10 per cent.	-	1,164,240
Property tax	-	249,543
		1,413,783

Profit - - - - 1,081,649

YEAR COMMENCING JANUARY 1815.

Former savings	- -	11,277,975
1814 - -	- -	1,081,649
		12,359,624
Bank notes	- -	27,300,000
Deposits -	- -	11,000,000
		50,659,624

Loan to Go- vernment }	3,000,000	
Cash and Bullion }	3,000,000	
	6,000,000	

44,659,624   2,232,980

Management of national debt,	250,000	
Loan - - -	28,800	
Life annuities - -	700	
Commission for receiving property tax	3,154	
	282,654	

Interest on capital - - - - 350,604

2,866,238

Expences - - -	300,000	
Stamps - - -	87,500	
	387,500	

2,478,738

Brought over - - - - - -   *L.*2,478,738

Dividend, 10 per cent. -   1,164,240

Property tax - - -   247,873

                                   1,412,113

             Profit - - -   1,066,625

JANUARY 1816.

Former savings - - - -   12,359,624

Savings, 1815 - - - -   1,066,625

                                 *L.*13,426,249

No. V

*Resolutions proposed concerning the Bank of England,
by Mr. Grenfell.*

1. That it appears, that there was paid by the public to
the Bank of England for managing the national debt, including the charge for contributions on loans and lotteries,
in the year ending 5th of July 1792, the sum of 99,803*l*.
12*s* 5*d*.; and that there was paid for the like service, in the
year ending 5th April 1815 the sum of 281,568*l*. 6*s*. 11¼*d*.;
being an increase of 181 754*l*. 14 6¼*d*. In addition to
which, the Bank of England have charged at the rate of
1250'. per million on the amount of property duty received
at the Bank on profits arising from professions, trades, and
offices.

2. That the total amount of Bank notes and Bank post
bills, in circulation in the years 1795 and 1796 (the latter
being the year previous to the restriction on cash payments,)
and in the year 1814, was as follows:

1795, 1st Feb. £12,735,520; and 1st Aug. £11,214,000.
1796, 1st Feb. 10,784,740; and 1st Aug.   9,856,110.
1814, 1st Feb. 25,154,950; and 1st Aug. 28,802,450.

3. That at present, and during many years past, more
particularly since the year 1806, considerable sums of public
money, forming together an average stationary balance
amounting to many millions, have been deposited with, or
otherwise placed in the custody of the Bank of England, acting in this respect as the bankers of the public.

4. That it appears, from a report ordered to be printed
10th of August 1807, from " the committee on the public
expenditure of the united kingdom," that the aggregate
amount of balances and deposits of public money in the hands
of the Bank of England, including Bank notes deposited in
the Exchequer, made up in four different periods of the
quarter ending 5th January 1807, fluctuated betwixt the sums

Vide Report, p. 74 & 75.
of £11,461,20? } including Bank notes deposited in
and 12,198,236 } the chests of the Exchequer.
or,
8,178,536 } excluding Bank notes deposited at
and 9,948,400 } the Exchequer.

5. That the aggregate amount of such deposits, together with the Exchequer bills and Bank notes deposited in the chests of the four tellers of the Exchequer, was, on an average, in the year 1814,

£11,966,371; including Bank notes deposited at the
or,   Exchequer, amounting to 642,264*l.*
11,324,107; excluding Bank notes deposited at the Exchequer.

6. That it appears, that this aggregate amount of deposits, together with such portions of the amount of Bank notes and Bank post bills in circulation as may have been invested by the Bank in securities bearing interest, was productive, during the same period, of interest and profit to the Bank of England.

7. That the only participation hitherto enjoyed by the public, since the year 1806, in the profits thus made on such deposits by the Bank, has consisted in a loan of three millions, advanced to the public by the Bank, by the 46 Geo. III. cap. 41., bearing 3 per cent. interest; which loan was discharged in December 1814: And in another loan of three millions, advanced to the public by the Bank, by the 48 Geo. III. cap. 3, free of any charge of interest; which loan became payable in December 1814, but has, by an act of the present session of parliament, cap. 16, been continued to the 5th of April 1816.

8. That this house will take into early consideration the advantages derived by the Bank, as well from the management of the national debt, as from the amount of balances of public money remaining in their hands, with the view to the adoption of such an arrangement, when the engagements now subsisting shall have expired, as may be consistent with what is due to the interests of the public, and to the rights, credit and stability, of the Bank of England.

13 *June* 1815.

No. VII.

Resolutions proposed concerning the Bank of England, by Mr. Mellish.

1. That by the act of 31 Geo. III. cap. 33, there was allowed to the Bank of England, for the management of the public debt, 450*l.* per million on the capital stock transferrable at the Bank, amounting in the year ending 5th July 1792, to 98,803*l.* 12*s.* 5*d.* on about 219,596,000*l.* then so transferrable; and that by the act 48 Geo. III. cap. 4, the said allowance was reduced to the rate of 340*l.* per million on all sums not exceeding 600 millions, and to 300*l.* per million on all sums exceeding that amount, whereby the Bank was entitled, in the year ending 5th April 1815, to the sum of 241,971*l.* 4*s.* 2¼*d.* on about 726,570,700*l.* capital stock, and 798*l.* 3*s.* 7*d.* on 2,347,588*l.*, 3 per cents. transferred for life annuities, being an increase of 143,965*l.* 15*s.* 4¼*d.* for management, and an increase of about 509,322,000*l.* capital stock: Also the Bank was allowed 1,000*l.* for taking in contributions, amounting to 812,500*l.* on a lottery in the year ending 5th July 1792; and 38,798*l.* 19*s.* 2*d.* for taking in contributions, amounting to 46,585,533*l.* 6*s.* 8*d.* on loans and lotteries in the year ending 5th April 1815.

2. That it appears, that the Bank, in pursuance of the act 46 Geo. III. cap. 65, has, from the year 1806 to the present time, made the assessments of the duty on profits arising from property, on the proprietors of the whole of the funded debt, transferrable at the Bank of England, and has deducted the said duty from each of the several dividend warrants, which in one year, ending 5th April 1815, amounted in number to 565,600; and that this part of the business has been done without any expense to, or charge on, the public.

That in pursuance of the abovementioned act, the duties so deducted have from time to time been placed to the " account of the commissioners of the treasury, on account of the said duties," together with other sums received from the public by virtue of the said act: part of this money is applied to the payment of certificates of allowances, and the remainder is paid into the Exchequer.

That by virtue of the said act, the lords commissioners of the treasury have made annual allowances, at the rate of

1,250*l.* per million, upon the amount so placed to the account of the commissioners of the treasury at the Bank of England, as a compensation for receiving, paying, and accounting for the same; which allowances, however, have not in any one year exceeded the sum of 3,480*l.*, and upon an average of eight years have amounted annually to 3,154*l.* only.

The amount of duties received for the year ending 5th April 1814, was 2,784 343*l.*, which, if it had been collected in the usual manner, at an allowance of 5*d.* per pound, would have cost the public 58,007*l.*; and the cost for collecting 20,188,293*l.*, being the whole of the duty received from 1806 to 1814, on which allowances have been made, would at the same rate have amounted to 420,589*l.*

That all monies received by the Bank on account of duties on property, are paid into the Exchequer immediately after the receipt thereof: when this circumstance is contrasted with the ordinary progress of monies into the exchequer, the advantage resulting to the public may be fairly estimated at 2*l.* per cent; which on the amount of duties for the year ending 5th April 1814, would be 55,686*l.*, and on the total amount from 1806 to 1814, would be 403,765*l.*

3. That the total amount of Bank notes and Bank post bills in circulation in the years 1795 and 1796, (the latter being the year previous to the restriction on cash payments) and in the year 1814, was as follows:

1795, 1st Feb. £12,735,520; . 1st Aug. £11,214,000.
1796, 1st Feb. 10,784,740; . 1st Aug. 9,856,110.
1814, 1st Feb. 25,154,950; . 1st Aug. 28,802,450.

4. That at present, and during many years past, both before and since the renewal of the charter of the Bank, considerable sums of the public money have been deposited with, or otherwise placed in the custody of the governor and company of the Bank of England, who act in this respect as the banker of the public. The average balances of these deposits, both before and after the renewal of the charter, were as follows:—

Public balances on an average of one year
   ending the 15th January 1800 . .   1,724,747.
Unclaimed dividends for the average of
   one year ending 1 Jan. 1800 . . .   837,966.

                         £2,562,713.

Public balances on an average of eight
    years, from 1807 to 1815 . . . .   4,375,405.
Unclaimed dividends . . . do. . .   634,614.

                            £5,010,019.

5. That it appears, from a report ordered to be printed
10th August 1807, from " the committee on public expenditure of the united kingdom," that the aggregate amount
of balances and deposits of public money in the Bank of
England, including Bank notes deposited in the Exchequer,
made up in four different periods of the quarter ending 5th
January 1807, fluctuated between the sums of 11,461,200*l.*
and 12,198,236*l.*; or, excluding Bank notes deposited at the
Exchequer, the amount fluctuated between 8,178,536*l.* and
9,948,400*l.*: the reason for which exclusion is not obvious,
as by the act of 48 Geo. III. cap. 3, the tellers of the Exchequer are authorized to take as securities on monies
lodged, either Exchequer bills, or notes of the governor and
company of the Bank of England. And it also appears, according to accounts laid before this house in the present session of parliament, that the aggregate amount of such deposits, together with the Exchequer bills and Bank notes deposited in the chests of the four tellers of the Exchequer,
was, on an average, in the year 1814,

£.11,966,371. Including Bank notes deposited at the
                Exchequer, amounting to 642,264*l.*
11,324,107. Excluding Bank notes deposited at the
                Exchequer.

6. That it appears, according to accounts before this
house, that the average of the aggregate amount of balances
of public money in the hands of the Bank of England, from
February 1807 to February 1815, was 5,010,019*l.*; and that
the average of bills and Bank notes deposited in the chests
of the four tellers of the Exchequer, from August 1807 to
April 1815, was 5,968 793*l.*; making together 10,978,812*l.*,
being 850,006*l.* less than the average of the said accounts
for one year ending 5th January 1807, as stated in the report
of the committee on the public expenditure.

7. That by the 39 & 40 Geo. III. cap. 28, extending the
charter of the Bank for twenty-one years, the Bank advanced to the public 3,000,000*l.* for six years without interest,

and extended the loan of 11,686,800*l.* for twenty-one years at an interest of 3*l.* per cent. per annum, as a consideration for the privileges, profits, emoluments, benefits and advantages, granted to the Bank by such extension of its charter.

That the interest of 3,000,000*l.* for six
years, at 5*l.* per cent. per annum, is £900,000.
That the difference between 3*l.* per cent.
and 5*l.* per cent. on 11,686,800*l.* is
233,736*l.*; which in twenty-one years
amounts to . . . . . 4,908,456.
That the above loan of 3,000,000*l.* was
continued to the public from 1806,
when it became payable, until 1814,
at an interest of 3*l.* per cent. making
an advantage in favour of the public
of 2*l.* per cent. or 60,000*l.* per annum;
which in eight years and eight months
amounts to . . . . . 520,000.
That in 1808 the Bank advanced to the
public 3,000,000*l.* without interest,
which by an act of the present session
is to remain without interest until the
5th of April 1816; the interest on this
advance, at 5*l.* per cent. will for eight
years amount to . . . . 1,200,000.

8. That by the 39 and 40 Geo. III. cap. 28, sec. 13, it is enacted, That during the continuance of the charter, the Bank shall enjoy all privileges, profits, emoluments, benefits and advantages whatsoever, which they now possess and enjoy by virtue of any employment by or on behalf of the public.

That previously to such renewal of their charter, the Bank was employed as the public banker, in keeping the cash of all the principal departments in the receipt of the public revenue, and in issuing and conducting the public expenditure.

That the average amount of the public
balances in the hands of the Bank, between the 1st February 1814, and the
15th January 1815, upon accounts
opened at the Bank previously to the

renewal of the charter on the 28th
March 1800, was   .   .   .   .   4,337,025.
Unclaimed dividends, for the average of
one year ending 1st January 1815 .   779,794.

                                      L.5,116,819

That the average public balances in the
hands of the Bank during the same period, upon accounts opened at the
Bank between the 28th March 1800
and the 27th Feb. 1808, was . .   *L.*370,018.
That the average public balances in the
hands of the Bank, during the same
period, upon accounts opened at the
Bank subsequent to the 27th February
1808, was .   .   .   .   261,162.

9. That whenever the engagements now subsisting between the public and the Bank shall expire, it may be proper to consider the advantages derived by the Bank from its
transactions with the public, with a view to the adoption of
such arrangements as may be consistent with those principles of equity and good faith, which ought to prevail in all
transactions between the public and the Bank of England.

26 *June,* 1815.

THE END.

In a few Days will be published,

THE SPEECH of PASCOE GRENFELL, Esq. delivered in the
House of Commons, on Tuesday, Feb. 13, 1816, on Transactions subsisting betwixt the Public and the Bank of England, with an Appendix of Official Documents. 8vo. 3s. 6d.

T. Davison, Lombard-street, Whitefriars, London.

Printed in the United States
By Bookmasters